HERSHEY'S®

Made | Simple™

Publications International, Ltd.

HERSHEY'S, HERSHEY'S trade dress, KISSES, KISSES Conical Configuration, HUGS, MAUNA LOA, HEATH, HEATH BITS 'O BRICKLE, MOUNDS, REESE'S, and SPECIAL DARK are trademarks used under license from The Hershey Company, Hershey, PA, 17033.

Made Simple is a trademark of Publications International, Ltd.

Front and back cover photography and photography on pages 7, 13, 21, 29, 43, 45, 55, 67, 73, 75, 79, 83, 86, 91, 103, 105, 107, 109, 111, 113, 115, 127, 135, 139, 141, and 145 by Stephen Hamilton Photographics, Inc, Chicago.

Photographers: Raymond Barrera, Jennifer Marx
Photographers' Assistants: Matt Savage, Jason McDonald
Prop Stylist: Andrea Kuhn
Food Stylists: Kathy Joy, Walter Moeller
Assistant Food Stylists: Elaine Funk, Jill Kaczanowski

Pictured on front cover: Fudge-Bottomed Chocolate Layer Pie *(page 90)*.

Pictured on back cover: Filled Chocolate Meringues *(page 6)*.

ISBN-13: 978-1-4127-9988-1

ISBN-10: 1-4127-9988-0

Library of Congress Control Number: 2008920413

Manufactured in China.

8 7 6 5 4 3 2 1

Microwave Cooking: Microwave ovens vary in wattage. Use the cooking times as guidelines and check for doneness before adding more time.

Contents

The Tradition Continues

We at Hershey's Kitchens have always been proud that our products are used by so many people in so many different ways. We are committed to supporting the imagination and creativity of chocolate lovers everywhere. This dedication goes back to Milton S. Hershey, the founder of our company and creator of our original products.

Milton S. Hershey, born in 1857 near Derry Church, Pennsylvania, began his confectionery career as an apprentice to a candy maker in Lancaster, Pennsylvania. In 1886 Mr. Hershey founded the business that established his candy-making reputation, the Lancaster Caramel Company.

In 1893, Mr. Hershey purchased German chocolate-making machinery and soon began producing chocolate coatings for his caramels. The Hershey Chocolate Company was born as a subsidiary of his Lancaster caramel business. Mr. Hershey also produced breakfast cocoa, sweet chocolate, and baking chocolate. After selling his caramel business to concentrate on chocolate, Mr. Hershey returned to his birthplace and began construction in 1903 on what is now the world's largest chocolate manufacturing plant, located in a town now known as Hershey, Pennsylvania.

This is still where we produce what Hershey is best known for: quality milk chocolate products. Since the 1920s, Hershey's Kitchens have created mouth-watering recipes featuring Hershey's ingredients that are known to create smiles and make mealtimes sweeter.

CLASSIC

Cookies & More

HERSHEY'S Easy Chocolate Cracker Snacks

Makes about 5½ dozen crackers

$1^2/_3$ cups (10-ounce package) HERSHEY'S Mint Chocolate Chips*

2 cups (12-ounce package) HERSHEY'S SPECIAL DARK Chocolate Chips or HERSHEY'S Semi-Sweet Chocolate Chips

2 tablespoons shortening (do not use butter, margarine, spread or oil)

60 to 70 round buttery crackers (about one-half 1-pound box)

*2 cups (11.5-ounce package) HERSHEY'S Milk Chocolate Chips and $1/_4$ teaspoon pure peppermint extract can be substituted for mint chocolate chips.

1. Line several trays or cookie sheets with wax paper.

2. Place mint chocolate chips, chocolate chips and shortening in large microwave-safe bowl. Microwave at MEDIUM (50%) 1 minute; stir. Continue heating 30 seconds at a time, stirring after each heating, until chips are melted and mixture is smooth when stirred.

3. Drop crackers into chocolate mixture one at a time. Using tongs, push cracker into chocolate so that it is covered completely. (If chocolate begins to thicken, reheat 10 to 20 seconds in microwave.) Remove from chocolate, tapping lightly on edge of bowl to remove excess chocolate. Place on prepared tray. Refrigerate until chocolate hardens, about 20 minutes. For best results, store tightly covered in refrigerator.

PEANUT BUTTER AND MILK CHOCOLATE: Use $1^2/_3$ cups (10-ounce package) REESE'S Peanut Butter Chips, 2 cups (11.5-ounce package) HERSHEY'S Milk Chocolate Chips and 2 tablespoons shortening. Proceed as directed.

WHITE CHIP AND TOFFEE: Melt 2 bags (12 ounces each) HERSHEY'S Premier White Chips and 2 tablespoons shortening. Dip crackers; before coating hardens sprinkle with HEATH BITS 'O BRICKLE Toffee Bits.

Filled Chocolate Meringues

Makes 2 dozen meringues

2 egg whites, at room temperature

1/4 teaspoon cream of tartar

Dash salt

1/2 cup sugar

1/2 teaspoon vanilla extract

2 tablespoons HERSHEY'S Cocoa

CHOCOLATE-CHEESE FILLING (recipe follows)

Raspberries and mint leaves for garnish

1. Heat oven to 275°F. Place parchment paper on cookie sheets.

2. Beat egg whites with cream of tartar and salt in medium bowl until soft peaks form. Beat in sugar, 1 tablespoon at a time, until stiff, glossy peaks form. Fold in vanilla. Sift cocoa over top of egg white mixture; gently fold in cocoa until combined. Drop by tablespoonfuls onto parchment paper. With back of small spoon, make indentation in center of each mound.

3. Bake 45 minutes or until meringue turns a light cream color and feels dry to the touch. Cool slightly; carefully peel meringues off parchment paper; cool completely on wire racks. To serve, spoon or pipe about 2 teaspoons CHOCOLATE-CHEESE FILLING into center of each meringue. Garnish each with a raspberry and a mint leaf.

CHOCOLATE-CHEESE FILLING: Combine 1 cup part-skim ricotta cheese, 2 tablespoons HERSHEY'S Cocoa, 1 tablespoon sugar and 1/2 teaspoon vanilla extract in food processor; blend until smooth. Cover; refrigerate. Makes 1 cup filling.

Marbled Cheesecake Bars

Makes 24 to 36 bars

CHOCOLATE CRUST
(recipe follows)

3 packages (8 ounces each) cream cheese, softened

1 can (14 ounces) sweetened condensed milk (not evaporated milk)

3 eggs

2 teaspoons vanilla extract

4 sections ($1/2$ ounce each) HERSHEY'S Unsweetened Chocolate Premium Baking Bar, melted

1. Prepare CHOCOLATE CRUST. Heat oven to 300°F.

2. Beat cream cheese in large bowl until fluffy. Gradually add sweetened condensed milk, beating until smooth. Add eggs and vanilla; mix well.

3. Pour half of batter evenly over prepared crust. Stir melted chocolate into remaining batter; drop by teaspoons over vanilla batter. With metal spatula or knife, swirl gently through batter to marble.

4. Bake 45 to 50 minutes or until set. Cool in pan on wire rack. Refrigerate several hours until chilled. Cut into bars. Cover; store leftover bars in refrigerator.

CHOCOLATE CRUST: Stir together 2 cups vanilla wafer crumbs (about 60 wafers), $1/3$ cup HERSHEY'S Cocoa and $1/2$ cup powdered sugar. Stir in $1/2$ cup (1 stick) melted butter or margarine until well blended. Press mixture firmly onto bottom of ungreased 13×9×2-inch baking pan.

Chocolate Orange Cheesecake Bars

Makes 24 bars

CRUST

1	cup all-purpose flour
1/2	cup packed light brown sugar
1/4	teaspoon ground cinnamon (optional)
1/3	cup shortening
1/2	cup chopped pecans

CHOCOLATE ORANGE FILLING

1	package (8 ounces) cream cheese, softened
2/3	cup granulated sugar
1/3	cup HERSHEY'S Cocoa
1/4	cup milk
1	egg
1	teaspoon vanilla extract
1/4	teaspoon freshly grated orange peel
	Pecan halves (optional)

1. Heat oven to 350°F.

2. For CRUST, stir together flour, brown sugar and cinnamon, if desired, in large bowl. Cut shortening into flour mixture with pastry blender or two knives until mixture resembles coarse crumbs. Stir in chopped pecans. Reserve 3/4 cup flour mixture. Press remaining mixture firmly onto bottom of ungreased 9-inch square baking pan. Bake 10 minutes or until lightly browned.

3. For CHOCOLATE ORANGE FILLING, beat cream cheese and granulated sugar with electric mixer on medium speed in medium bowl until fluffy. Add cocoa, milk, egg, vanilla and orange peel; beat until smooth.

4. Spread filling over warm crust. Sprinkle with reserved flour mixture. Press pecan halves lightly onto top, if desired. Return to oven. Bake 25 to 30 minutes or until lightly browned. Cool; cut into bars. Cover; refrigerate leftover bars.

Double Peanut Butter Paisley Brownies

About 36 brownies

1/2 cup (1 stick) butter or margarine, softened

1/4 cup REESE'S Creamy Peanut Butter

1 cup granulated sugar

1 cup packed light brown sugar

3 eggs

1 teaspoon vanilla extract

2 cups all-purpose flour

2 teaspoons baking powder

1/4 teaspoon salt

1 2/3 cups (10-ounce package) REESE'S Peanut Butter Chips

1/2 cup HERSHEY'S Syrup or HERSHEY'S SPECIAL DARK Syrup

1. Heat oven to 350°F. Grease 13×9×2-inch baking pan.

2. Beat butter and peanut butter in large bowl. Add granulated sugar and brown sugar; beat well. Add eggs, one at a time, beating well after each addition. Blend in vanilla.

3. Stir together flour, baking powder and salt; mix into peanut butter mixture, blending well. Stir in peanut butter chips. Spread half of batter in prepared pan; spoon syrup over top. Carefully spread with remaining batter; swirl with metal spatula or knife for marbled effect.

4. Bake 35 to 40 minutes or until lightly browned. Cool completely in pan on wire rack. Cut into squares.

REESE'S Peanut Butter and Milk Chocolate Chip Tassies

Makes 3 dozen cookies

3/4 cup (1 1/2 sticks) butter, softened

1 package (3 ounces) cream cheese, softened

1 1/2 cups all-purpose flour

3/4 cup sugar, divided

1 egg, slightly beaten

2 tablespoons butter or margarine, melted

1/4 teaspoon lemon juice

1/4 teaspoon vanilla extract

1 cup HERSHEY'S Milk Chocolate Chips

1 cup REESE'S Peanut Butter Chips

2 teaspoons shortening (do not use butter, margarine, spread or oil)

1. Beat 3/4 cup butter and cream cheese in medium bowl; add flour and 1/4 cup sugar, beating until well blended. Cover; refrigerate about one hour or until dough is firm. Shape dough into 1-inch balls; press balls onto bottoms and up sides of about 36 small muffin cups (1 3/4 inches in diameter).

2. Heat oven to 350°F. Combine egg, remaining 1/2 cup sugar, melted butter, lemon juice and vanilla in small bowl; stir until smooth. Stir together milk chocolate chips and peanut butter chips. Set aside 1/3 cup chip mixture; add remaining chips to egg mixture. Evenly fill muffin cups with egg mixture.

3. Bake 20 to 25 minutes or until filling is set and lightly browned. Cool completely; remove from pan to wire rack.

4. Combine remaining 1/3 cup chip mixture and shortening in small microwave-safe bowl. Microwave at MEDIUM (50%) 30 seconds; stir. If necessary, microwave additional 10 seconds at a time, stirring after each heating, until chips are melted and mixture is smooth when stirred. Drizzle over tops of tassies.

Peanut Butter Fudge Brownie Bars

Makes 36 bars

1 cup (2 sticks) butter or margarine, melted

1 1/2 cups sugar

2 eggs

1 teaspoon vanilla extract

1 1/4 cups all-purpose flour

2/3 cup HERSHEY'S Cocoa

1/4 cup milk

1 1/4 cups chopped pecans or walnuts, divided

1/2 cup (1 stick) butter or margarine

1 2/3 cups (10-ounce package) REESE'S Peanut Butter Chips

1 can (14 ounces) sweetened condensed milk (not evaporated milk)

1/4 cup HERSHEY'S SPECIAL DARK Chocolate Chips or HERSHEY'S Semi-Sweet Chocolate Chips

1. Heat oven to 350°F. Grease 13×9×2-inch baking pan.

2. Beat melted butter, sugar, eggs and vanilla in large bowl with electric mixer on medium speed until well blended. Add flour, cocoa and milk; beat until blended. Stir in 1 cup nuts. Spread in prepared pan.

3. Bake 25 to 30 minutes or just until edges begin to pull away from sides of pan. Cool completely in pan on wire rack.

4. Melt 1/2 cup butter and peanut butter chips in medium saucepan over low heat, stirring constantly. Add sweetened condensed milk, stirring until smooth; pour over baked layer.

5. Place chocolate chips in small microwave-safe bowl. Microwave at MEDIUM (50%) 45 seconds or just until chips are melted when stirred. Drizzle bars with melted chocolate; sprinkle with remaining 1/4 cup nuts. Refrigerate 1 hour or until firm. Cut into bars. Cover; refrigerate leftover bars.

Chocolate-Cherry Slice 'n' Bake Cookies

Makes about 7½ dozen cookies

3/4 cup (1½ sticks) butter or margarine, softened

1 cup sugar

1 egg

1½ teaspoons vanilla extract

2¼ cups all-purpose flour

2 teaspoons baking powder

1/2 teaspoon salt

1/4 cup finely chopped maraschino cherries

1/2 teaspoon almond extract

Red food color

1/3 cup HERSHEY'S Cocoa

1/4 teaspoon baking soda

4 teaspoons water

COCOA ALMOND GLAZE (recipe follows)

1. Beat butter, sugar, egg and vanilla in large bowl until fluffy. Stir together flour, baking powder and salt; gradually add to butter mixture, beating until mixture forms a smooth dough. Remove 1¼ cups dough to medium bowl; blend in cherries, almond extract and about 6 drops food color.

2. Stir together cocoa and baking soda. Add with water to remaining dough; blend until smooth. Divide chocolate dough in half; roll each half between two sheets of wax paper, forming 12×4½-inch rectangle. Remove top sheet of wax paper. Divide cherry mixture in half; with floured hands, shape each half into 12-inch roll. Place one roll in center of each rectangle; wrap chocolate dough around roll, forming one large roll. Wrap in plastic wrap. Refrigerate about 6 hours or until firm.

3. Heat oven to 350°F.

4. Cut rolls into 1/4-inch-thick slices; place on ungreased cookie sheet. Bake 7 minutes or until set. Cool 1 minute; remove from cookie sheet to wire rack. Cool completely. Prepare COCOA ALMOND GLAZE; decorate cookies.

Cocoa Almond Glaze

2 tablespoons butter or margarine

2 tablespoons HERSHEY'S Cocoa

2 tablespoons water

1 cup powdered sugar

1/8 teaspoon almond extract

Melt butter in small saucepan over low heat. Add cocoa and water; stir constantly until mixture thickens. Do not boil. Remove from heat. Add powdered sugar and almond extract, beating until smooth and of desired consistency. Add additional water, 1/2 teaspoon at a time, if needed. Makes about 1/2 cup glaze.

Cranberry Orange Ricotta Cheese Brownies

Makes about 16 brownies

$^1/_2$ cup (1 stick) butter or margarine, melted

$^3/_4$ cup sugar

1 teaspoon vanilla extract

2 eggs

$^3/_4$ cup all-purpose flour

$^1/_2$ cup HERSHEY'S Cocoa

$^1/_2$ teaspoon baking powder

$^1/_2$ teaspoon salt

CHEESE FILLING (recipe follows)

1. Heat oven to 350°F. Grease 9-inch square baking pan.

2. Stir together butter, sugar and vanilla in medium bowl; add eggs, beating well. Stir together flour, cocoa, baking powder and salt; add to butter mixture, mixing thoroughly. Spread half of chocolate batter in prepared pan. Spread CHEESE FILLING over top. Drop remaining chocolate batter by teaspoonfuls onto cheese filling.

3. Bake 40 to 45 minutes or until wooden pick inserted in center comes out clean. Cool completely in pan on wire rack. Cut into squares. Refrigerate leftover brownies.

Cheese Filling

1 cup ricotta cheese

$^1/_4$ cup sugar

3 tablespoons whole-berry cranberry sauce

2 tablespoons cornstarch

1 egg

$^1/_4$ to $^1/_2$ teaspoon freshly grated orange peel

4 drops red food color (optional)

Beat ricotta cheese, sugar, cranberry sauce, cornstarch and egg in small bowl until smooth. Stir in orange peel and food color, if desired.

Chocolate Toffee Crunch Squares

Makes 3 dozen squares

4 cups (two 11.5-ounce packages) HERSHEY'S Milk Chocolate Chips

1 cup HEATH BITS 'O BRICKLE Toffee Bits

1 cup salted peanuts

1 cup halved pretzel sticks

1/2 cup MOUNDS Sweetened Coconut Flakes (optional)

1/2 cup HERSHEY'S Premier White Chips

1 teaspoon shortening (do not use butter, margarine, spread or oil)

Paper candy cups (optional)

1. Line 9-inch square pan with plastic wrap. Place chocolate chips in large microwave-safe bowl. Microwave at MEDIUM (50%) 1 minute; stir. If necessary, microwave at MEDIUM an additional 15 seconds at a time, stirring after each heating just until chips are melted and mixture is smooth when stirred. Immediately add toffee bits, peanuts, pretzels and coconut, if desired; stir to coat.

2. Spread mixture in prepared pan; cover with plastic wrap or foil. Refrigerate 45 minutes or until firm.

3. Place white chips and shortening in small microwave-safe bowl. Microwave at MEDIUM (50%) 30 seconds; stir. If necessary, microwave at MEDIUM an additional 10 seconds at a time, stirring after each heating just until chips are melted and mixture is smooth when stirred. Using fork, drizzle white chips mixture over chocolate mixture in pan. Cover; refrigerate 5 minutes or until firm.

4. Bring to room temperature. Remove chocolate mixture from pan and place right-side up on cutting board; remove plastic wrap. Cut into 1 1/2-inch squares. Place each square in a candy cup, if desired. Store in covered container in a cool place.

VARIATION **CHOCOLATE TOFFEE HAYSTACKS**

Prepare chocolate mixture as above. Instead of spreading into square pan, drop chocolate mixture by slightly heaping tablespoons onto wax paper-lined cookie sheet or tray. Refrigerate until firm. Melt white chips as direct above; drizzle over haystacks.

Mini Brownie Cups

Makes 24 servings

1/4 cup (1/2 stick) light margarine

2 egg whites

1 egg

3/4 cup sugar

2/3 cup all-purpose flour

1/3 cup HERSHEY'S Cocoa

1/2 teaspoon baking powder

1/4 teaspoon salt

MOCHA GLAZE
(recipe follows)

1. Heat oven to 350°F. Line small muffin cups (1 3/4 inches in diameter) with paper bake cups or spray with vegetable cooking spray.

2. Melt margarine in small saucepan over low heat; cool slightly. Beat egg whites and egg in small bowl with electric mixer on medium speed until foamy; gradually add sugar, beating until slightly thickened and light in color. Stir together flour, cocoa, baking powder and salt; gradually add to egg mixture, beating until blended. Gradually add melted margarine, beating just until blended. Fill muffin cups 2/3 full with batter.

3. Bake 15 to 18 minutes or until wooden pick inserted in center comes out clean. Remove from pan to wire rack. Cool completely. Prepare MOCHA GLAZE; drizzle over tops of brownie cups. Let stand until glaze is set.

Mocha Glaze

1/4 cup powdered sugar

3/4 teaspoon HERSHEY'S Cocoa

1/4 teaspoon powdered instant coffee

2 teaspoons hot water

1/4 teaspoon vanilla extract

Stir together powdered sugar and cocoa in small bowl. Dissolve coffee in water; gradually add to sugar mixture, stirring until well blended. Stir in vanilla.

Layered Apricot Snacking Bars

Makes about 16 bars

2 cups (12-ounce package) HERSHEY'S Premier White Chips, divided

1 package (6 ounces) dried apricots, cut into 1/4-inch pieces

1 cup boiling water

1/2 cup (1 stick) margarine, softened

1/3 cup granulated sugar

1/4 cup packed light brown sugar

1 egg

1 teaspoon vanilla extract

1 cup plus 2 tablespoons all-purpose flour, divided

1/4 teaspoon baking soda

1/4 teaspoon salt

1/2 cup wheat germ

2 tablespoons honey

1 egg white

1/2 teaspoon shortening (do not use butter, margarine, spread or oil)

1. Heat oven to 350°F.

2. Measure 1/3 cup white chips for glaze; set aside. Stir together apricots and water in small bowl; cover. Let stand 5 minutes; drain. Meanwhile, in large bowl, beat margarine, granulated sugar, brown sugar, egg and vanilla until well blended.

3. Stir together 1 cup flour, baking soda and salt; gradually add to margarine mixture, beating until well blended. Stir in remaining 1 2/3 cups white chips; press mixture onto bottom of ungreased 8-inch square baking pan. Spread softened apricots over cookie base. Stir together wheat germ, remaining 2 tablespoons flour, honey and egg white until blended; crumble over apricots.

4. Bake 30 to 35 minutes or until wheat germ and edges are lightly browned. Cool completely in pan on wire rack.

5. Stir together reserved white chips and shortening in small microwave-safe bowl. Microwave at MEDIUM (50%) 30 seconds; stir. If necessary, microwave at MEDIUM an additional 10 seconds at a time, stirring after each heating, just until chips are melted when stirred. Using tines of fork, drizzle mixture over top; let stand until glaze is firm. Cut into bars.

Peanut Butter Cut-Out Cookies

Makes about 3 dozen cookies

1/2	cup (1 stick) butter or margarine
1	cup REESE'S Peanut Butter Chips
2/3	cup packed light brown sugar
1	egg
3/4	teaspoon vanilla extract
1 1/3	cups all-purpose flour
3/4	teaspoon baking soda
1/2	cup finely chopped pecans
	CHOCOLATE CHIP GLAZE (recipe follows)

1. Place butter and peanut butter chips in medium saucepan; cook over low heat, stirring constantly, until melted. Pour into large bowl; add brown sugar, egg and vanilla, beating until well blended. Stir in flour, baking soda and pecans, blending well. Refrigerate 15 to 20 minutes or until firm enough to roll.

2. Heat oven to 350°F.

3. Roll a small portion of dough at a time on lightly floured board, or between 2 pieces of wax paper, to 1/4-inch thickness. (Keep remaining dough in refrigerator.) With cookie cutters, cut dough into desired shapes; place on ungreased cookie sheets.

4. Bake 7 to 8 minutes or until almost set (do not overbake). Cool 1 minute; remove from cookie sheets to wire racks. Cool completely. Drizzle CHOCOLATE CHIP GLAZE onto each cookie; allow to set.

CHOCOLATE CHIP GLAZE: Place 1 cup HERSHEY'S SPECIAL DARK Chocolate Chips or HERSHEY'S Semi-Sweet Chocolate Chips and 1 tablespoon shortening (do not use butter, margarine spread or oil) in small microwave-safe bowl. Microwave at MEDIUM (50%) 1 minute; stir. If necessary, microwave at MEDIUM an additional 15 seconds at a time, stirring after each heating, just until chips are melted and mixture is smooth.

Cinnamon Chips Gems

Makes 4 dozen cookies

1 cup (2 sticks) butter or margarine, softened

2 packages (3 ounces each) cream cheese, softened

2 cups all-purpose flour

1/2 cup sugar

1/3 cup ground toasted almonds

2 eggs

1 can (14 ounces) sweetened condensed milk

1 teaspoon vanilla extract

1 1/3 cups HERSHEY'S Cinnamon Chips, divided

1. Beat butter and cream cheese in large bowl until well blended; stir in flour, sugar and almonds. Cover; refrigerate about 1 hour.

2. Divide dough into 4 equal parts. Shape each part into 12 smooth balls. Place each ball in small muffin cup (1 3/4 inches in diameter); press evenly on bottom and up side of each cup.

3. Heat oven to 375°F. Beat eggs in small bowl. Add sweetened condensed milk and vanilla; mix well. Place 7 cinnamon chips in bottom of each cookie shell; fill a generous 3/4 full with sweetened condensed milk mixture.

4. Bake 18 to 20 minutes or until tops are puffed and just beginning to turn golden brown. Cool 3 minutes. Sprinkle about 15 chips on top of each cookie. Cool completely in pan on wire rack. Remove from pan using small metal spatula or sharp knife. Store tightly covered at room temperature.

Chocolate Cranberry Bars

Makes 36 bars

2 cups vanilla wafer crumbs (about 60 wafers, crushed)

1/2 cup HERSHEY'S Cocoa

3 tablespoons sugar

2/3 cup cold butter, cut into pieces

1 can (14 ounces) sweetened condensed milk (not evaporated milk)

1 cup REESE'S Peanut Butter Chips

1 1/3 cups (6-ounce package) sweetened dried cranberries or 1 1/3 cups raisins

1 cup coarsely chopped walnuts

1. Heat oven to 350°F.

2. Stir together vanilla wafer crumbs, cocoa and sugar in medium bowl; cut in butter until crumbly. Press mixture evenly on bottom and 1/2 inch up sides of 13×9×2-inch baking pan. Pour sweetened condensed milk evenly over crumb mixture; sprinkle evenly with peanut butter chips and dried cranberries. Sprinkle nuts on top; press down firmly.

3. Bake 25 to 30 minutes or until lightly browned. Cool completely in pan on wire rack. Cover with foil; let stand several hours before cutting into bars and serving.

Design Your Own Chocolate Cookie

Makes about 5 dozen cookies

1 cup (2 sticks) butter, softened

1 cup granulated sugar

3/4 cup packed light brown sugar

2 teaspoons vanilla extract

1/2 teaspoon salt

2 eggs

2 cups all-purpose flour

1/2 cup HERSHEY'S Cocoa

1 teaspoon baking soda

1. Heat oven to 375°F.

2. Beat butter, granulated sugar, brown sugar, vanilla and salt in large bowl until creamy. Add eggs; beat well.

3. Stir together flour, cocoa and baking soda; gradually add to butter mixture, beating until well blended. Drop by rounded teaspoons onto ungreased cookie sheet.

4. Bake 8 to 10 minutes or until set. Cool slightly; remove from cookie sheet to wire rack. Cool completely.

CHOCOLATE CHOCOLATE CHIP COOKIES: Add 2 cups (one 12- or 11.5-ounce package) HERSHEY'S Mini-Chips Semi-Sweet Chocolate, HERSHEY'S SPECIAL DARK or Milk Chocolate Chips to basic chocolate batter.

MINI KISSES CHOCOLATE COOKIES: Add 1 3/4 cups (10-ounce package) HERSHEY'S MINI KISSES BRAND Milk Chocolates to basic chocolate batter.

MINT CHOCOLATE CHIP COOKIES: Add 1 2/3 cups (10-ounce package) HERSHEY'S Mint Chocolate Chips to basic chocolate batter.

CHOCOLATE COOKIES WITH WHITE CHIPS: Add 2 cups (12-ounce package) HERSHEY'S Premier White Chips to basic chocolate batter.

CHOCOLATE COOKIES WITH PEANUT BUTTER CHIPS: Add 1 2/3 cups (10-ounce package) REESE'S Peanut Butter Chips to basic chocolate batter

CHOCOLATE COOKIES WITH TOFFEE: Add 1 to 1 1/4 cups HEATH BITS 'O BRICKLE Toffee Bits or HEATH Milk Chocolate Toffee Bits to basic chocolate batter. Lightly grease or paper-line cookie sheets.

California Chocolate Bars

Makes about 16 bars

6 tablespoons butter or margarine, softened

1/2 cup granulated sugar

1/4 cup packed light brown sugar

1 egg

1 teaspoon freshly grated orange peel

1 teaspoon vanilla extract

1 cup all-purpose flour

1/2 teaspoon baking soda

1/4 teaspoon salt

1/2 cup chopped dried apricots

1/2 cup coarsely chopped walnuts

1 cup HERSHEY'S MINI KISSES BRAND Milk Chocolates

MILK CHOCOLATE GLAZE (recipe follows, optional)

1. Heat oven to 350°F. Grease 9-inch square baking pan.

2. Beat butter, granulated sugar, brown sugar and egg in large bowl until fluffy. Add orange peel and vanilla; beat until blended. Stir together flour, baking soda and salt; add to orange mixture. Stir in apricots, walnuts and chocolates; spread in prepared pan.

3. Bake 25 to 30 minutes or until lightly browned and bars begin to pull away from sides of pan. Cool completely in pan on wire rack. Prepare MILK CHOCOLATE GLAZE, if desired; drizzle over top. Allow to set; cut into bars.

MILK CHOCOLATE GLAZE: Place 1/4 cup HERSHEY'S MINI KISSES BRAND Milk Chocolates and 3/4 teaspoon shortening (do not use butter, margarine, spread or oil) in small microwave-safe bowl. Microwave at MEDIUM (50%) 45 seconds or until chocolates are melted and mixture is smooth when stirred.

Peanut Butter Chip Fruit Bars

Makes 24 bars

1 1/2 cups REESE'S Peanut Butter Chips, divided

1 package (8 ounces) cream cheese, softened

1 cup packed light brown sugar

1 egg

1 teaspoon vanilla extract

1 cup all-purpose flour

1/2 teaspoon baking soda

1/4 teaspoon salt

1/2 cup quick-cooking oats

1 cup chopped dried mixed fruit or dried fruit bits

1 cup powdered sugar

2 tablespoons orange juice

1/4 teaspoon freshly grated orange peel (optional)

1. Heat oven to 350°F. Grease 13×9×2-inch baking pan.

2. Place 1 cup peanut butter chips in microwave-safe bowl. Microwave at MEDIUM (50%) 1 minute; stir. If necessary, microwave an additional 15 seconds at a time, stirring after each heating, until chips are melted and smooth when stirred. Beat melted peanut butter chips and cream cheese in large bowl until well blended. Add brown sugar, egg and vanilla; blend well. Stir together flour, baking soda and salt; add to cream cheese mixture, blending well. Stir in oats, remaining 1/2 cup peanut butter chips and dried fruit.

3. Spread batter in prepared pan. Bake 20 to 25 minutes or until golden brown. Cool in pan on wire rack.

4. Meanwhile, stir together powdered sugar, orange juice and grated orange peel in small mixing bowl; blend until smooth. (Add additional orange juice, a teaspoonful at a time, if glaze is too thick.) Pour over bars and cool completely. Cut into bars.

Double Striped Peanut Butter Oatmeal Cookies

About 4 dozen cookies

$1/4$ cup REESE'S Creamy Peanut Butter

$1/2$ cup (1 stick) butter or margarine, softened

$1/3$ cup granulated sugar

$1/3$ cup packed light brown sugar

1 egg

2 tablespoons milk

1 teaspoon vanilla extract

$1 1/4$ cups quick-cooking oats, divided

1 cup all-purpose flour

1 teaspoon baking soda

$1/2$ teaspoon salt

$1/2$ cup HERSHEY'S Milk Chocolate Chips

2 teaspoons shortening (do not use butter, margarine, spread or oil)

$1/2$ cup REESE'S Peanut Butter Chips

1. Heat oven to 350°F. Beat peanut butter and butter in large bowl until well blended. Add granulated sugar and brown sugar; beat until fluffy. Add egg, milk and vanilla; beat well. Stir together $1/2$ cup oats, flour, baking soda and salt; gradually beat into peanut butter mixture.

2. Shape dough into 1-inch balls. Roll in remaining oats; place on ungreased cookie sheet. Flatten cookies with tines of fork to form a crisscross pattern.

3. Bake 10 to 12 minutes or until lightly browned. Cool slightly; remove from cookie sheet to wire rack. Cool completely.

4. Place chocolate chips and 1 teaspoon shortening in medium microwave-safe container. Microwave at MEDIUM (50%) 30 seconds; stir. If necessary, microwave an additional 10 seconds at a time, stirring after each heating, until chocolate is melted and smooth when stirred. Drizzle over cookies. Repeat procedure with peanut butter chips and remaining 1 teaspoon shortening. Allow drizzles to set.

S'mores Sandwich Bar Cookies

Makes 16 bars

$^1/_2$ cup (1 stick) butter or margarine, softened

$^3/_4$ cup sugar

1 egg

1 teaspoon vanilla extract

$1^1/_3$ cups all-purpose flour

$^3/_4$ cup graham cracker crumbs

1 teaspoon baking powder

$^1/_4$ teaspoon salt

$1^1/_3$ cups (8-ounce package) HERSHEY'S Mini Milk Chocolate Bars or 5 HERSHEY'S Milk Chocolate Bars (1.55 ounce each)

3 cups miniature marshmallows

1. Heat oven to 350°F. Grease 8-inch square baking pan.

2. Beat butter and sugar in large bowl until well blended. Add egg and vanilla; beat well. Stir together flour, graham cracker crumbs, baking powder and salt; add to butter mixture, beating until blended. Press half of dough into prepared pan. Bake 15 minutes.

3. Sprinkle mini chocolate bars over baked layer or arrange unwrapped chocolate bars over baked layer, breaking as needed to fit. Sprinkle with marshmallows; scatter bits of remaining dough over marshmallows, forming top layer. Bake 10 to 15 minutes or just until lightly browned. Cool completely in pan on wire rack. Cut into bars.

Pecan MINI KISSES Cups

Makes 24 cups

1/2 cup (1 stick) butter or margarine, softened

1 package (3 ounces) cream cheese, softened

1 cup all-purpose flour

1 egg

2/3 cup packed light brown sugar

1 tablespoon butter, melted

1 teaspoon vanilla extract

Dash salt

72 HERSHEY'S MINI KISSES BRAND Milk Chocolates, divided

1/2 to 3/4 cup coarsely chopped pecans

1. Beat 1/2 cup softened butter and cream cheese in medium bowl until blended. Add flour; beat well. Cover; refrigerate about 1 hour or until firm enough to handle.

2. Heat oven to 325°F. Stir together egg, brown sugar, 1 tablespoon melted butter, vanilla and salt in small bowl until well blended.

3. Shape chilled dough into 24 balls (1 inch each). Place balls in ungreased small muffin cups (1 3/4 inches in diameter). Press onto bottoms and up sides of cups. Place 2 chocolate pieces in each cup. Spoon about 1 teaspoon pecans over chocolate. Fill each cup with egg mixture.

4. Bake 25 minutes or until filling is set. Lightly press 1 chocolate into center of each cookie. Cool in pan on wire rack.

TIP Use HERSHEY'S MINI KISSES BRAND Milk Chocolates to decorate cakes, cupcakes, cookies and pies. Stir into slightly softened ice cream or sprinkle over top of a sundae for an added chocolate taste treat.

Cappuccino-Kissed Cheesecake
Makes 16 servings

1½ cups chocolate cookie crumbs

6 tablespoons butter or margarine, melted

1¼ cups HERSHEY'S MINI KISSES BRAND Milk Chocolates, divided

4 packages (8 ounces each) cream cheese, softened

²/₃ cup sugar

3 eggs

¹/₃ cup milk

1 tablespoon instant espresso powder

¹/₄ teaspoon ground cinnamon

ESPRESSO CREAM (recipe follows)

1. Heat oven to 350°F. Combine cookie crumbs and butter; press onto bottom and 1 inch up side of 9-inch springform pan.

2. Melt 1 cup chocolate pieces in small saucepan over low heat, stirring constantly. Combine cream cheese and sugar in large bowl, beating on medium speed of mixer until well blended. Add eggs, milk, espresso powder and cinnamon; beat on low speed until well blended. Add melted chocolate pieces; beat on medium 2 minutes. Spoon mixture into crust.

3. Bake 55 minutes. Remove from oven to wire rack. Cool 15 minutes; with knife, loosen cake from side of pan. Cool completely; remove side of pan. Cover; refrigerate at least 4 hours before serving.

4. To serve, garnish with ESPRESSO CREAM and remaining ¹/₄ cup chocolates. Cover; refrigerate leftover cheesecake.

ESPRESSO CREAM: Beat ¹/₂ cup cold whipping cream, 2 tablespoons powdered sugar and 1 teaspoon instant espresso powder until stiff.

KISSES Fluted Cups with Peanut Butter Filling

Makes about 2 dozen pieces

72 HERSHEY'S KISSES BRAND Milk Chocolates, divided

1 cup REESE'S Creamy Peanut Butter

1 cup powdered sugar

1 tablespoon butter or margarine, softened

1. Line 24 small muffin cups (1 3/4 inches in diameter) with small paper bake cups. Remove wrappers from chocolates.

2. Place 48 chocolates in small microwave-safe bowl. Microwave at MEDIUM (50%) 1 minute; stir. Microwave at MEDIUM an additional 10 seconds at a time, stirring after each heating, just until chocolate is melted when stirred. Using small brush, coat inside of paper cups with melted chocolate.

3. Refrigerate 20 minutes; reapply melted chocolate to any thin spots. Refrigerate until firm, preferably overnight. Gently peel paper from chocolate cups.

4. Beat peanut butter, powdered sugar and butter with electric mixer on medium speed in small bowl until smooth. Spoon into chocolate cups. Before serving, top each cup with a chocolate piece. Cover; store cups in refrigerator.

Secret KISSES Cookies

Makes 3 dozen cookies

1 cup (2 sticks) butter or margarine, softened

1/2 cup granulated sugar

1 teaspoon vanilla extract

1 3/4 cups all-purpose flour

1 cup finely chopped walnuts or almonds

36 HERSHEY'S KISSES BRAND Milk Chocolates or HERSHEY'S KISSES BRAND Milk Chocolates with Almonds

Powdered sugar

1. Beat butter, granulated sugar and vanilla with electric mixer on medium speed in large bowl until fluffy. Add flour and walnuts; beat on low speed of mixer until well blended. Cover; refrigerate 1 to 2 hours or until dough is firm enough to handle.

2. Remove wrappers from chocolates. Heat oven to 375°F. Using about 1 tablespoon dough for each cookie, shape dough around each chocolate; roll in hand to make ball. (Be sure to cover each chocolate piece completely.) Place on ungreased cookie sheet.

3. Bake 10 to 12 minutes or until cookies are set but not browned. Cool slightly; remove to wire rack. While still slightly warm, roll in powdered sugar. Cool completely. Store in tightly covered container. Roll again in powdered sugar just before serving.

VARIATION Sift together 1 tablespoon HERSHEY'S Cocoa with 1/3 cup powdered sugar. Roll warm cookies in cocoa mixture.

KISSES Chocolate Mousse

Makes 4 servings

36 HERSHEY'S KISSES BRAND Milk Chocolates

1 1/2 cups miniature marshmallows or 15 regular marshmallows

1/3 cup milk

2 teaspoons kirsch (cherry brandy) or 1/4 teaspoon almond extract

6 to 8 drops red food color (optional)

1 cup cold whipping cream

Additional HERSHEY'S KISSES BRAND Milk Chocolates (optional)

1. Remove wrappers from chocolates. Combine marshmallows and milk in small saucepan. Cook over low heat, stirring constantly, until marshmallows are melted and mixture is smooth. Remove from heat.

2. Pour 1/3 cup marshmallow mixture into medium bowl; stir in brandy and food color, if desired. Set aside. To remaining marshmallow mixture, add 36 chocolates; return to low heat, stirring constantly until chocolate is melted. Remove from heat; cool to room temperature.

3. Beat whipping cream in small bowl until stiff. Fold 1 cup whipped cream into chocolate mixture. Gradually fold remaining whipped cream into reserved mixture. Fill 4 parfait glasses about 3/4 full with chocolate mousse; spoon or pipe reserved marshmallow mixture on top. Refrigerate 3 to 4 hours or until set. Garnish with additional chocolates, if desired.

HERSHEY'S Double Chocolate Cheesecake

Makes about 20 squares

$1/2$ cup (1 stick) butter or margarine, softened

$1 1/4$ cups sugar, divided

$1/4$ teaspoon salt

1 cup all-purpose flour

$1/4$ cup HERSHEY'S Cocoa

2 packages (8 ounces each) cream cheese, softened

2 eggs

2 teaspoons vanilla extract

$1/2$ cup HERSHEY'S Mini Chips Semi-Sweet Chocolate

18 HERSHEY'S KISSES BRAND Milk Chocolates

Sweetened whipped cream (optional)

Additional HERSHEY'S KISSES BRAND Milk Chocolates (optional)

1. Heat oven to 350°F. Line 8- or 9-inch springform pan* with foil, extending edges over pan sides.

2. Beat butter, $1/2$ cup sugar and salt in small bowl until smooth. Stir together flour and cocoa; gradually add to butter mixture, beating on low speed of mixer until soft dough is formed. Press dough onto bottom of prepared pan.

3. Beat cream cheese and remaining $3/4$ cup sugar in medium bowl until smooth. Add eggs and vanilla; beat until well blended. Remove 1 cup batter; set aside. Add small chocolate chips to remaining batter; pour over crust.

4. Remove wrappers from 18 chocolates; place in medium microwave-safe bowl. Microwave at MEDIUM (50%) 1 minute; stir. If necessary, microwave at MEDIUM an additional 15 seconds at a time, stirring after each heating, until chocolate is melted and smooth when stirred. Add to reserved batter, stirring until well blended. Drop by spoonfuls onto batter in pan; gently swirl with knife or spatula for marbled effect.

5. Bake 35 to 40 minutes or until cheesecake is firm and top is slightly puffed. Cool completely in pan on wire rack. Cover; refrigerate several hours until chilled. To serve, lift from pan using foil edges; cut into squares. Garnish each square with whipped cream and chocolate pieces, if desired. Cover; refrigerate leftover cheesecake.

NOTE *8- or 9-inch square baking pan can also be used.

KISSES Macaroon Cookies

Makes about 4 dozen cookies

1/3 cup butter or margarine, softened

1 package (3 ounces) cream cheese, softened

3/4 cup sugar

1 egg yolk

2 teaspoons almond extract

2 teaspoons orange juice

1 1/4 cups all-purpose flour

2 teaspoons baking powder

1/4 teaspoon salt

5 cups MOUNDS Sweetened Coconut Flakes, divided

48 HERSHEY'S KISSES BRAND Milk Chocolates

1. Beat butter, cream cheese and sugar with electric mixer on medium speed in large bowl until well blended. Add egg yolk, almond extract and orange juice; beat well. Stir together flour, baking powder and salt; gradually add to butter mixture. Stir in 3 cups coconut. Cover; refrigerate 1 hour or until firm enough to handle. Meanwhile, remove wrappers from chocolates.

2. Heat oven to 350°F.

3. Shape dough into 1-inch balls; roll in remaining 2 cups coconut. Place on ungreased cookie sheet.

4. Bake 10 to 12 minutes or until lightly browned. Immediately press chocolate piece into center of each cookie. Cool 1 minute. Carefully remove to wire rack and cool completely.

HERSHEY'S Double Chocolate MINI KISSES Cookies

Makes about 3½ dozen cookies

1 cup (2 sticks) butter or margarine, softened

1½ cups sugar

2 eggs

2 teaspoons vanilla extract

2 cups all-purpose flour

²/3 cup HERSHEY'S Cocoa

³/4 teaspoon baking soda

¹/4 teaspoon salt

1³/4 cups (10-ounce package) HERSHEY'S MINI KISSES BRAND Milk Chocolates

¹/2 cup coarsely chopped nuts (optional)

1. Heat oven to 350°F.

2. Beat butter, sugar, eggs and vanilla with electric mixer on medium speed in large bowl until light and fluffy. Stir together flour, cocoa, baking soda and salt; add to butter mixture, beating until well blended. Stir in chocolates and nuts, if desired. Drop by tablespoons onto ungreased cookie sheet.

3. Bake 8 to 10 minutes or just until set. Cool slightly. Remove to wire rack and cool completely.

HERSHEY'S KISSES Birthday Cake

Makes 10 to 12 servings

2 cups sugar

1$3/4$ cups all-purpose flour

$3/4$ cup HERSHEY'S Cocoa
or HERSHEY'S SPECIAL
DARK Cocoa

1$1/2$ teaspoons baking powder

1$1/2$ teaspoons baking soda

1 teaspoon salt

2 eggs

1 cup milk

$1/2$ cup vegetable oil

2 teaspoons vanilla extract

1 cup boiling water

VANILLA BUTTERCREAM
FROSTING
(recipe follows)

HERSHEY'S KISSES BRAND
Milk Chocolates

1. Heat oven to 350°F. Grease and flour two 9-inch round baking pans or one 13×9×2-inch baking pan.

2. Stir together sugar, flour, cocoa, baking powder, baking soda and salt in large bowl. Add eggs, milk, oil and vanilla; beat with electric mixer on medium speed for 2 minutes. Stir in boiling water (batter will be thin). Pour batter into prepared pans.

3. Bake 30 to 35 minutes for round pans, 35 to 40 minutes for rectangular pan or until wooden pick inserted in center comes out clean. Cool 10 minutes; turn out onto wire racks. Cool completely.

4. Frost with VANILLA BUTTERCREAM FROSTING. Remove wrappers from chocolates. Garnish top and sides of cake with chocolates.

Vanilla Buttercream Frosting

$1/3$ cup butter or margarine, softened

4 cups powdered sugar, divided

3 to 4 tablespoons milk

1$1/2$ teaspoons vanilla extract

Beat butter with electric mixer on medium speed in large bowl until creamy. With mixer running, gradually add about 2 cups powdered sugar, beating until well blended. Slowly beat in milk and vanilla. Gradually add remaining powdered sugar, beating until smooth. Add additional milk, if necessary, until frosting is desired consistency. Makes about 2$1/3$ cups frosting.

HUGS & KISSES Crescents

Makes 8 crescents

1 package (8 ounces) refrigerated crescent dinner rolls

24 HERSHEY'S KISSES BRAND Milk Chocolates or HERSHEY'S HUGS Candies

Powdered sugar

1. Heat oven to 375°F. Separate dough into 8 triangles. Remove wrappers from chocolates.

2. Place 2 chocolates at center of wide end of each triangle; place an additional chocolate on top of other two pieces. Starting at wide end, roll to opposite point; pinch edges to seal. Place rolls, pointed side down, on ungreased cookie sheet. Curve into crescent shape.

3. Bake 10 minutes or until lightly browned. Cool slightly; sift with powdered sugar. Serve warm.

NOTE Leftover crescents can be reheated in microwave for a few seconds.

Peanut Butter Blossoms

Makes about 4 dozen cookies

48 HERSHEY'S KISSES BRAND Milk Chocolates

$3/4$ cup REESE'S Creamy Peanut Butter

$1/2$ cup shortening

$1/3$ cup granulated sugar

$1/3$ cup packed light brown sugar

1 egg

2 tablespoons milk

1 teaspoon vanilla extract

$1 1/2$ cups all-purpose flour

1 teaspoon baking soda

$1/2$ teaspoon salt

Granulated sugar

1. Heat oven to 375°F. Remove wrappers from chocolates.

2. Beat peanut butter and shortening with electric mixer on medium speed in large bowl until well blended. Add $1/3$ cup granulated sugar and brown sugar; beat until fluffy. Add egg, milk and vanilla; beat well. Stir together flour, baking soda and salt; gradually beat into peanut butter mixture.

3. Shape dough into 1-inch balls. Roll in additional granulated sugar; place on ungreased cookie sheet.

4. Bake 8 to 10 minutes or until lightly browned. Immediately press a chocolate into center of each cookie; cookies will crack around edges. Remove to wire racks and cool completely.

REESE'S Peanut Butter & HERSHEY'S KISSES Pie

Makes 8 servings

About 42 HERSHEY'S KISSES BRAND Milk Chocolates, divided

2 tablespoons milk

1 packaged (8-inch) crumb crust (6 ounces)

1 package (8 ounces) cream cheese, softened

3/4 cup sugar

1 cup REESE'S Creamy Peanut Butter

1 tub (8 ounces) frozen non-dairy whipped topping, thawed and divided

1. Remove wrappers from chocolates. Place 26 chocolates and milk in small microwave-safe bowl. Microwave at MEDIUM (50%) 1 minute or just until melted and smooth when stirred. Spread evenly on bottom of crust. Refrigerate about 30 minutes.

2. Beat cream cheese with electric mixer on medium speed in medium bowl until smooth; gradually beat in sugar, then peanut butter, beating well after each addition. Reserve 1/2 cup whipped topping; fold remaining whipped topping into peanut butter mixture. Spoon into crust over chocolate. Cover; refrigerate about 6 hours or until set.

3. Garnish with reserved whipped topping and remaining chocolates. Cover; refrigerate leftover pie.

Shower Them with KISSES Cake

Makes 24 servings

2 packages (18¹/₄ ounces each) white cake mix, divided

2¹/₂ cups water, divided

²/₃ cup vegetable oil, divided

4 eggs

¹/₂ cup sugar, divided

¹/₄ cup HERSHEY'S Cocoa, divided

PREMIER WHITE BUTTERCREAM FROSTING (recipe follows)

CHOCOLATE BUTTERCREAM FROSTING (recipe follows)

2 packages (10 ounces each) HERSHEY'S MINI KISSES BRAND Milk Chocolate

MILK CHOCOLATE FILIGREE HEARTS (recipe follows)

1. Heat oven to 350°F. Grease and flour 8-inch square baking pan and 8-inch round baking pan. Line bottoms with wax paper; grease and flour paper.

2. Place contents of 1 package cake mix, 1¹/₄ cups water, ¹/₃ cup vegetable oil and 2 eggs in large bowl; beat until blended. Place 1 cup batter in small bowl; stir in ¹/₄ cup sugar and 2 tablespoons cocoa until blended. Divide vanilla batter evenly into prepared pans; spoon cocoa batter in dollops over top of batter in pans. With knife or spatula, marble chocolate through vanilla batter.

3. Bake 30 to 35 minutes or until wooden pick inserted in center comes out clean. Cool 15 minutes; remove cakes from pans. Remove wax paper; cool completely.

4. Repeat steps 1, 2 and 3.

5. Prepare PREMIER WHITE BUTTERCREAM FROSTING and CHOCOLATE BUTTERCREAM FROSTING. To assemble cake, cover 18×14-inch heavy cardboard with foil. Cut both round layers in half vertically. Arrange 1 square and 2 semi-circles into heart shape. Spread with small amount of frosting; place other square and 2 semi-circles on top. Frost top with white frosting; frost sides with chocolate frosting. Outline entire top and bottom edges of heart-shaped cake with chocolate pieces. Garnish with MILK CHOCOLATE FILIGREE HEARTS, if desired.

Premier White Buttercream Frosting

2 cups (12-ounce package) HERSHEY'S Premier White Chips

¹/₃ cup milk

1¹/₂ cups (3 sticks) cold butter, cut into pieces

1³/₄ cups powdered sugar

1. Place white chips and milk in large microwave-safe bowl. Microwave at MEDIUM (50%) 1 minute; stir. If necessary, microwave an additional 15 seconds at a time, until mixture is melted and smooth when stirred; cool to lukewarm.

2. Beat butter and powdered sugar gradually into white chip mixture; beat until fluffy. Makes about 4 cups frosting.

Chocolate Buttercream Frosting

In bowl, place 2 cups of PREMIER WHITE BUTTERCREAM FROSTING; beat in 2 tablespoons HERSHEY'S Cocoa.

Milk Chocolate Filigree Hearts

1 cup HERSHEY'S MINI KISSES BRAND Milk Chocolates

1. Draw desired size heart shapes on paper; cover with wax paper. Place both sheets of paper on baking sheet or tray.

2. Place chocolate pieces in microwave-safe bowl. Microwave at MEDIUM (50%) 30 seconds or just until chocolate is melted when stirred.

3. Pour melted chocolate in small, heavy seal-top plastic bag. With scissors, make small diagonal cut in bottom corner of bag. Pipe thick outlines of heart shapes following heart outlines; fill in center of hearts with a crisscross of chocolate to connect the sides. Refrigerate until firm.

4. Carefully peel wax paper away from chocolate hearts. Place on tray; cover and refrigerate until ready to use as garnishes for cake.

Thick and Fudgey Brownies with HERSHEY'S MINI KISSES Milk Chocolates

Makes 24 brownies

2¹/4 cups all-purpose flour

²/3 cup HERSHEY'S Cocoa

1 teaspoon baking powder

1 teaspoon salt

³/4 cup (1¹/2 sticks) butter or margarine, melted

2¹/2 cups sugar

2 teaspoons vanilla extract

4 eggs

1³/4 cups (10-ounce package) HERSHEY'S MINI KISSES BRAND Milk Chocolates

1. Heat oven to 350°F. (325°F. for glass baking dish). Grease 13×9×2-inch baking pan.

2. Stir together flour, cocoa, baking powder and salt. With spoon or whisk, stir together butter, sugar and vanilla in large bowl. Add eggs; stir until well blended. Stir in flour mixture, blending well. Stir in chocolate pieces. Spread batter in prepared pan.

3. Bake 30 to 35 minutes or until brownies begin to pull away from sides of pan. Cool completely in pan on wire rack; cut into 2-inch squares.

HERSHEY'S Triple Chocolate Cookies

Makes about 4 dozen cookies

48 HERSHEY'S KISSES BRAND Milk Chocolates or HERSHEY'S KISSES BRAND Milk Chocolates with Almonds

$1/2$ cup (1 stick) butter or margarine, softened

$3/4$ cup granulated sugar

$3/4$ cup packed light brown sugar

1 teaspoon vanilla extract

2 eggs

1 tablespoon milk

$2^{1}/4$ cups all-purpose flour

$1/3$ cup HERSHEY'S Cocoa

1 teaspoon baking soda

$1/2$ teaspoon salt

1 cup HERSHEY'S SPECIAL DARK Chocolate Chips or HERSHEY'S Semi-Sweet Chocolate Chips

1. Remove wrappers from chocolates. Heat oven to 350°F.

2. Beat butter, granulated sugar, brown sugar and vanilla with electric mixer on medium speed in large bowl until well blended. Add eggs and milk; beat well.

3. Stir together flour, cocoa, baking soda and salt; gradually beat into butter mixture, beating until well blended. Stir in chocolate chips. Shape dough into 1-inch balls. Place on ungreased cookie sheet.

4. Bake 10 to 11 minutes or until set. Gently press a chocolate into center of each cookie. Remove to wire rack and cool completely.

VARIATION For vanilla cookies, omit cocoa and add an additional $1/3$ cup all-purpose flour.

SPECIAL DARK
Delights

REESE'S Peanut Butter Bark

About 1 pound candy

2 packages (4 ounces each)
HERSHEY'S SPECIAL
DARK Chocolate
Premium Baking Bar,
broken into pieces

1²/₃ cups (10-ounce package)
REESE'S Peanut Butter
Chips

1 tablespoon shortening
(do not use butter,
margarine, spread or oil)

¹/₂ cup coarsely roasted
peanuts or toasted
almonds,* coarsely
chopped

*To toast almonds: Heat oven
to 350°F. Spread almonds in
thin layer in shallow baking
pan. Bake 8 to 10 minutes,
stirring occasionally, until light
golden brown; cool.

1. Cover tray with wax paper.

2. Place chocolate in medium microwave-safe bowl.
Microwave at MEDIUM (50%) 1 minute; stir. If necessary,
microwave at MEDIUM an additional 30 seconds at a time,
stirring after each heating, until chocolate is melted and
smooth when stirred.

3. Immediately place peanut butter chips and shortening
in second microwave-safe bowl. Microwave at MEDIUM
1 minute; stir. If necessary, microwave at MEDIUM an
additional 30 seconds at a time, stirring after each heating,
until chips are melted and mixture is smooth when stirred;
stir in peanuts.

4. Alternately spoon above mixtures onto prepared tray;
swirl with knife for marbled effect. Cover; refrigerate until
firm. Break into pieces.

HERSHEY'S SPECIAL DARK Chocolate
Layered Cheesecake

Makes 10 to 12 servings

CHOCOLATE CRUMB
CRUST (recipe follows)

3 packages (8 ounces each)
cream cheese, softened

3/4 cup sugar

4 eggs

1/4 cup heavy cream

2 teaspoons vanilla extract

1/4 teaspoon salt

2 cups (12-ounce package)
HERSHEY'S SPECIAL
DARK Chocolate Chips,
divided

1/2 teaspoon shortening
(do not use butter,
margarine, spreads or oil)

1. Prepare CHOCOLATE CRUMB CRUST. Heat oven to 350°F.

2. Beat cream cheese and sugar in large bowl until smooth. Gradually beat in eggs, heavy cream, vanilla and salt, beating until well blended; set aside.

3. Set aside 2 tablespoons chocolate chips. Place remaining chips in large microwave-safe bowl. Microwave at MEDIUM (50%) 1 1/2 minutes; stir. If necessary, microwave at MEDIUM an additional 15 seconds at a time, stirring after each heating, until chocolate is melted when stirred.

4. Gradually blend 1 1/2 cups cheesecake batter into melted chocolate. Spread 2 cups chocolate mixture in prepared crust.

5. Blend another 2 cups plain cheesecake batter into remaining chocolate mixture; spread 2 cups of this mixture over first layer. Stir remaining cheesecake batter into remaining chocolate mixture; spread over second layer.

6. Bake 50 to 55 minutes or until center is almost set. Remove from oven to wire rack. With knife, immediately loosen cake from side of pan. Cool to room temperature.

7. Place reserved chocolate chips and shortening in small microwave-safe bowl. Microwave at MEDIUM 30 seconds; stir. If necessary, microwave at MEDIUM an additional 10 seconds at a time, stirring after each heating, until chocolate is melted and smooth when stirred. Drizzle over top of cheesecake. Cover; refrigerate several hours until cold. Cover and refrigerate leftover cheesecake.

CHOCOLATE CRUMB CRUST: Stir together 1 1/2 cups vanilla wafer crumbs (about 45 wafers), 1/2 cup powdered sugar and 1/4 cup HERSHEY'S Cocoa; stir in 1/4 cup (1/2 stick) melted butter or margarine. Press mixture onto bottom and 1 1/2 inches up sides of 9-inch springform pan.

HERSHEY'S SPECIAL DARK Snack Cake Medley

Makes 12 to 16 servings

CREAM CHEESE FILLING
(recipe follows)

3 cups all-purpose flour

2 cups sugar

2/3 cup HERSHEY'S Cocoa

2 teaspoons baking soda

1 teaspoon salt

2 cups water

2/3 cup vegetable oil

2 eggs

2 tablespoons white vinegar

2 teaspoons vanilla extract

1/2 cup HERSHEY'S SPECIAL
DARK Chocolate Chips

1/2 cup MOUNDS Sweetened
Coconut Flakes

1/2 cup chopped nuts

1. Heat oven to 350°F. Grease and flour 13×9×2-inch baking pan. Prepare CREAM CHEESE FILLING; set aside.

2. Stir together flour, sugar, cocoa, baking soda and salt in large bowl. Add water, oil, eggs, vinegar and vanilla; beat on medium speed of mixer 2 minutes or until well blended. Pour 3 cups batter into prepared pan. Gently drop cream cheese filling onto batter by heaping teaspoonfuls. Carefully spoon remaining batter over filling. Combine chocolate chips, coconut and nuts; sprinkle over top of batter.

3. Bake 50 to 55 minutes or until wooden pick inserted into cake center comes out almost clean and cake starts to crack slightly. Cool completely in pan on wire rack. Cover and store leftover cake in refrigerator.

Cream Cheese Filling

1/2 cup HERSHEY'S SPECIAL DARK Chocolate Chips

1 package (8 ounces) cream cheese, softened

1/3 cup sugar

1 egg

1/2 teaspoon vanilla extract

1. Place chocolate chips in small microwave-safe bowl. Microwave at MEDIUM (50%) 30 seconds; stir. If necessary, microwave an additional 10 seconds at a time, stirring after each heating, until chips are melted and smooth when stirred.

2. Beat cream cheese and sugar in medium bowl until well blended. Beat in egg and vanilla. Add melted chocolate, beating until well blended.

Berry-Berry Brownie Torte

Makes 8 to 10 servings

1/2 cup all-purpose flour

1/4 teaspoon baking soda

1/4 teaspoon salt

1 cup HERSHEY'S SPECIAL DARK Chocolate Chips or HERSHEY'S Semi-Sweet Chocolate Chips

1/2 cup (1 stick) butter or margarine

1 1/4 cups sugar, divided

2 eggs

1 teaspoon vanilla extract

1/3 cup HERSHEY'S SPECIAL DARK Cocoa

1/2 cup whipping cream

3/4 cup fresh blackberries, rinsed and patted dry

3/4 cup fresh raspberries, rinsed and patted dry

1. Heat oven to 350°F. Line 9-inch round baking pan with wax paper, then grease. Stir together flour, baking soda and salt. Stir in chocolate chips.

2. Melt butter in medium saucepan over low heat. Remove from heat. Stir in 1 cup sugar, eggs and vanilla. Add cocoa, blending well. Stir in flour mixture. Spread mixture in prepared pan.

3. Bake 20 to 25 minutes or until wooden pick inserted into center comes out slightly sticky. Cool in pan on wire rack 15 minutes. Invert onto wire rack; remove wax paper. Turn right side up; cool completely.

4. Beat whipping cream and remaining 1/4 cup sugar until sugar is dissolved and stiff peaks form. Spread over top of brownie. Top with berries. Refrigerate until serving time.

Chocolate Seven Layer Bars

Makes 36 bars

1¹/₂ cups finely crushed thin pretzels or pretzel sticks

³/₄ cup (1¹/₂ sticks) butter or margarine, melted

1 can (14 ounces) sweetened condensed milk (not evaporated milk)

1 package (4 ounces) HERSHEY'S Unsweetened Chocolate Premium Baking Bar, broken into pieces

2 cups miniature marshmallows

1 cup MOUNDS Sweetened Coconut Flakes

1 cup coarsely chopped pecans

1 package (4 ounces) HERSHEY'S SPECIAL DARK Chocolate Premium Baking Bar, broken into pieces

1 tablespoon shortening (do not use butter, margarine, spread or oil)

1. Heat oven to 350°F. Combine pretzels and melted butter in small bowl; press evenly onto bottom of ungreased 13×9×2-inch baking pan.

2. Place sweetened condensed milk and unsweetened chocolate in small microwave-safe bowl. Microwave at MEDIUM (50%) 1 minute; stir. If necessary, microwave at MEDIUM an additional 15 seconds at a time, stirring after each heating, until mixture is melted and smooth when stirred. Carefully pour over pretzel layer in pan. Top with marshmallows, coconut and pecans; press firmly down onto chocolate layer.

3. Bake 25 to 30 minutes or until lightly browned; cool completely in pan on wire rack.

4. Melt SPECIAL DARK chocolate and shortening in small microwave-safe bowl at MEDIUM (50%) 1 minute or until melted when stirred; drizzle over entire top. Cut into bars. Refrigerate 15 minutes or until glaze is set.

HERSHEY'S SPECIAL DARK Truffle Brownie Cheesecake

Makes 10 to 12 servings

SPECIAL DARK
DELIGHTS

Brownie Layer

6	tablespoons melted butter or margarine
1 1/4	cups sugar
1	teaspoon vanilla extract
2	eggs
1	cup plus 2 tablespoons all-purpose flour
1/3	cup HERSHEY'S Cocoa
1/2	teaspoon baking powder
1/2	teaspoon salt

Truffle Cheesecake Layer

3	packages (8 ounces each) cream cheese, softened
3/4	cup sugar
4	eggs
1/4	cup heavy cream
2	teaspoons vanilla extract
1/4	teaspoon salt
2	cups (12-ounce package) HERSHEY'S SPECIAL DARK Chocolate Chips, divided
1/2	teaspoon shortening (do not use butter, margarine, spread or oil)

1. Heat oven to 350°F. Grease 9-inch springform pan.

2. For BROWNIE LAYER, stir together melted butter, 1 1/4 cups sugar and 1 teaspoon vanilla. Add 2 eggs; stir until blended. Stir in flour, cocoa, baking powder and 1/2 teaspoon salt; blend well. Spread in prepared pan. Bake 25 to 30 minutes or until brownie layer pulls away from sides of pan.

3. Meanwhile for TRUFFLE CHEESECAKE LAYER, beat cream cheese and 3/4 cup sugar with electric mixer on medium speed in large bowl until smooth. Gradually beat in 4 eggs, heavy cream, 2 teaspoons vanilla and 1/4 teaspoon salt until well blended.

4. Set aside 2 tablespoons chocolate chips. Place remaining chips in large microwave-safe bowl. Microwave at MEDIUM (50%) 1 1/2 minutes or until chips are melted and smooth when stirred. Gradually blend melted chocolate into cheesecake batter.

5. Remove BROWNIE LAYER from oven and immediately spoon cheesecake mixture over brownie. Return to oven; continue baking 45 to 50 minutes or until center is almost set. Remove from oven to wire rack. With knife, loosen cake from side of pan. Cool to room temperature. Remove side of pan.

6. Place remaining 2 tablespoons chocolate chips and shortening in small microwave-safe bowl. Microwave at MEDIUM (50%) 30 seconds or until chips are melted and mixture is smooth when stirred. Drizzle over top of cheesecake. Cover; refrigerate several hours until cold. Garnish as desired. Cover and refrigerate leftover cheesecake.

80

SPECIAL DARK Chocolate Chip Scones

Makes 24 scones

3¹/4 cups all-purpose flour

¹/2 cup sugar

1 tablespoon plus
1 teaspoon baking
powder

¹/4 teaspoon salt

2 cups (12-ounce package)
HERSHEY'S SPECIAL
DARK Chocolate Chips

¹/2 cup chopped nuts
(optional)

2 cups whipping cream,
chilled

2 tablespoons butter,
melted

Additional sugar

Powdered sugar
(optional)

1. Heat oven to 375°F. Lightly grease 2 baking sheets.

2. Stir together flour, ¹/2 cup sugar, baking powder and salt in large bowl. Stir in chocolate chips and nuts, if desired.

3. Stir whipping cream into flour mixture just until ingredients are moistened.

4. Turn mixture out onto lightly floured surface. Knead gently until soft dough forms, about 2 minutes. Divide dough into three equal balls. One ball at a time, flatten into 7-inch circle; cut into 8 triangles. Transfer triangles to prepared baking sheets, spacing 2 inches apart. Brush with melted butter and sprinkle with additional sugar.

5. Bake 15 to 20 minutes or until lightly browned. Serve warm, sprinkled with powdered sugar, if desired.

European Mocha Fudge Cake

Makes 10 to 12 servings

SPECIAL DARK DELIGHTS

1^1/$_4$ cups (2^1/$_2$ sticks) butter or margarine

^{3}/$_4$ cup HERSHEY'S SPECIAL DARK Cocoa

4 eggs

^{1}/$_4$ teaspoon salt

1 teaspoon vanilla extract

2 cups sugar

1 cup all-purpose flour

1 cup finely chopped pecans

CREAMY COFFEE FILLING (recipe follows)

Chocolate curls (optional)

1. Heat oven to 350°F. Butter bottom and sides of two 9-inch round baking pans. Line bottoms with wax paper; butter paper.

2. Melt butter in small saucepan; remove from heat. Add cocoa, stirring until blended; cool slightly. Beat eggs in large bowl until foamy; add salt and vanilla. Gradually add sugar, beating well. Add cooled chocolate mixture; blend thoroughly. Fold in flour. Stir in pecans. Pour mixture into prepared pans.

3. Bake 20 to 25 minutes or until wooden pick inserted in center comes out clean. Do not overbake. Cool 5 minutes; remove from pans to wire racks. Carefully peel off paper. Cool completely. Spread CREAMY COFFEE FILLING between layers, over top and sides of cake. Garnish with chocolate curls, if desired. Refrigerate 1 hour or longer before serving.

Creamy Coffee Filling

1^1/$_2$ cups cold whipping cream

^{1}/$_3$ cup packed light brown sugar

2 teaspoons powdered instant coffee

Combine all ingredients; stir until coffee is almost dissolved. Beat until stiff. About 3 cups filling.

MAKE AHEAD DIRECTIONS Cooled cake may be wrapped and frozen up to 4 weeks; thaw, wrapped, before filling and frosting.

Chocolate and Vanilla-Swirled Cheese Pie

Makes 8 servings

2 packages (8 ounces each) cream cheese, softened

1/2 cup sugar

1 teaspoon vanilla extract

2 eggs

1 prepared deep-dish crumb crust (9 ounces)

1 cup HERSHEY'S SPECIAL DARK Chocolate Chips

1/4 cup milk

Red raspberry jam (optional)

1. Heat oven to 350°F.

2. Beat cream cheese, sugar and vanilla in mixer bowl until well blended. Add eggs; mix thoroughly. Spread 2 cups batter in crumb crust.

3. Place chocolate chips in medium microwave-safe bowl. Microwave at MEDIUM (50%) 1 minute; stir. If necessary, microwave an additional 15 seconds at a time, stirring after each heating, until chocolate is melted and smooth when stirred. Cool slightly. Add melted chocolate and milk to remaining batter; blend thoroughly. Drop chocolate batter by tablespoonfuls onto vanilla batter. Gently swirl with knife for marbled effect.

4. Bake 30 to 35 minutes or until center is almost set. Cool; refrigerate several hours or overnight. Drizzle with warmed red raspberry jam, if desired. Cover and refrigerate leftover pie.

HERSHEY'S SPECIAL DARK Chips and Macadamia Nut Fudge

Makes about 5 dozen pieces or about 2¼ pounds candy

1³/₄ cups sugar

1 jar (7 ounces) marshmallow crème

³/₄ cup evaporated milk

¹/₄ cup (¹/₂ stick) butter

2²/₃ cups (two 8-ounce packages) HERSHEY'S SPECIAL DARK Chips and Macadamia Pieces

1 teaspoon vanilla extract

1. Line 8-inch square pan with foil, extending foil over edges of pan.

2. Combine sugar, marshmallow crème, evaporated milk and butter in heavy 3-quart saucepan. Cook over medium heat, stirring constantly, until mixture comes to a full boil; boil and stir 5 minutes.

3. Remove from heat. Gradually add chips and nuts, stirring until chips are melted. Stir in vanilla. Pour into prepared pan; cool until set.

4. Remove from pan; place on cutting board. Peel off foil. Cut into squares. Store tightly covered in cool, dry place.

NOTE For best results, do not double this recipe.

SPECIAL DARK DELIGHTS

Fudge-Bottomed Chocolate Layer Pie

Makes 6 to 8 servings

1   cup HERSHEY'S SPECIAL
    DARK Chocolate Chips,
    divided

2   tablespoons plus $1/4$ cup
    milk, divided

1   packaged chocolate
    crumb crust (6 ounces)

$1^1/_2$ cups miniature
    marshmallows

1   tub (8 ounces) frozen
    nondairy whipped
    topping, thawed and
    divided

    Additional sweetened
    whipped cream or
    whipped topping
    (optional)

1. Place $1/3$ cup chocolate chips and 2 tablespoons milk in microwave-safe bowl. Microwave 30 seconds at MEDIUM (50%); stir. If necessary, microwave an additional 15 seconds at a time, stirring after each heating, until chips are melted and mixture is smooth when stirred. Spread on bottom of crust. Refrigerate while preparing next step.

2. Place marshmallows, remaining $2/3$ cup chocolate chips and remaining $1/4$ cup milk in small saucepan. Cook over medium heat, stirring constantly, until marshmallows are melted and mixture is well blended. Transfer to separate large bowl; cool completely.

3. Stir 2 cups whipped topping into cooled chocolate mixture; spread 2 cups mixture over chocolate in crust. Blend remaining whipped topping and remaining chocolate mixture; spread over surface of pie.

4. Cover; freeze several hours or until firm. Garnish as desired. Cover and freeze leftover pie.

SPECIAL DARK Fudge Fondue

Makes 1½ cups

2 cups (12-ounce package)
HERSHEY'S SPECIAL
DARK Chocolate Chips

½ cup light cream

2 teaspoons vanilla extract

Assorted fondue dippers
such as marshmallows,
cherries, grapes,
mandarin orange
segments, pineapple
chunks, strawberries,
slices of other fresh
fruits, small pieces of
cake or small brownies

1. Place chocolate chips and light cream in medium microwave-safe bowl. Microwave at MEDIUM (50%) 1 minute or just until chips are melted and mixture is smooth when stirred. Stir in vanilla.

2. Pour into fondue pot or chafing dish; serve warm with fondue dippers. If mixture thickens, stir in additional light cream, one tablespoon at a time. Refrigerate leftover fondue.

STOVETOP DIRECTIONS Combine chocolate chips and light cream in heavy medium saucepan. Cook over low heat, stirring constantly, until chips are melted and mixture is hot. Stir in vanilla and continue as in Step 2 above.

Mocha Molten Chocolate Cake

Makes 4 individual (6-ounce) cakes

FROZEN CHOCOLATE
(recipe follows)

2 teaspoons instant coffee granules

1/4 cup water

1 cup all-purpose flour

1/2 cup plus 1 tablespoon HERSHEY'S Cocoa

1/8 teaspoon salt

3/4 cup (1 1/2 sticks) plus 2 tablespoons butter, softened

1 1/4 cups sugar, divided

2 teaspoons vanilla extract

3 eggs

MOCHA CREAM (recipe follows)

1. Prepare FROZEN CHOCOLATE.

2. Heat oven to 425°F. Butter sides and bottom of four 6-ounce ramekins. Place on baking sheet.

3. Dissolve coffee granules in water; set aside. Stir together flour, cocoa and salt; set aside.

4. Beat butter in large bowl with electric mixer until light and fluffy. Set aside 1 tablespoon sugar; gradually beat in remaining sugar, vanilla and dissolved coffee, beating thoroughly.

5. Separate egg yolks from the egg whites. One at a time, add egg yolks to butter mixture, beating well after each addition.

6. In separate bowl, beat egg whites at low speed until frothy. Gradually increasing to high speed, beat the whites until soft peaks start to form. Add remaining tablespoon sugar, one teaspoon at a time, beating until stiff, shiny peaks form.

7. Fold one-third of the cocoa mixture and one-third of the egg whites into the butter mixture. One-half at a time, gently fold remaining cocoa mixture and egg whites into mixture.

8. Spoon about 2/3 cup batter into each ramekin. Place heaping teaspoon FROZEN CHOCOLATE mixture on center of each batter-filled ramekin. Spoon about 1/4 cup of remaining batter over FROZEN CHOCOLATE making sure to cover completely.

9. Bake 15 to 20 minutes or until tops have started to crack.

10. While cakes are baking reheat remaining FROZEN CHOCOLATE and make MOCHA CREAM.

11. To serve, carefully invert cake onto large dinner plate. Spoon MOCHA CREAM around base of cake; dust with powdered sugar. Garnish as desired. Serve immediately with the warmed chocolate sauce.

Frozen Chocolate

1	cup HERSHEY'S SPECIAL DARK Chocolate Chips
1	teaspoon instant coffee granules
3/4	cup heavy cream
2	tablespoons light corn syrup
1	teaspoon vanilla extract

Place chocolate chips and coffee granules in medium mixing bowl. Stir together cream and corn syrup in medium saucepan. Cook over medium heat, stirring constantly with wooden spoon, until mixture comes to a boil. Pour hot cream over chocolate, let stand 30 seconds; stir until chocolate is melted and mixture is smooth. Stir in vanilla. Pour chocolate mixture into shallow bowl or dish. Cool slightly. Freeze at least 3 to 4 hours (mixture will not freeze completely).

Mocha Cream

1	cup whipping cream
3	tablespoons powdered sugar
1	tablespoon HERSHEY'S Cocoa
2	teaspoons instant coffee granules
1	teaspoon vanilla extract

Beat cream, powdered sugar, cocoa, coffee granules and vanilla in small mixer bowl until cream starts to thicken, but is still pourable. Do not overbeat.

Chocolate Squares with Nutty Caramel Sauce

Makes 9 servings

1 cup sugar

3/4 cup all-purpose flour

1/2 cup HERSHEY'S SPECIAL DARK Cocoa or HERSHEY'S Cocoa

1/2 teaspoon baking powder

1/2 teaspoon salt

3/4 cup vegetable oil

3 eggs

1/4 cup milk

1/2 teaspoon vanilla extract

1 bag (14 ounces) caramel candies

1/2 cup water

1 cup pecan pieces

Sweetened whipped cream (optional)

1. Heat oven to 350°F. Grease bottom only of 8-inch square baking pan.

2. Stir together sugar, flour, cocoa, baking powder and salt in medium bowl. Add oil, eggs, milk and vanilla; beat until smooth. Pour batter into prepared pan.

3. Bake 35 to 40 minutes or until wooden pick inserted in center comes out clean. Cool completely in pan on wire rack.

4. Remove wrappers from caramels. Combine caramels and water in small saucepan. Cook over low heat, stirring occasionally, until smooth and well blended. Stir in pecans; cool until thickened slightly. Cut cake into squares; serve with warm caramel nut sauce and sweetened whipped cream, if desired.

Peanut Butter Fudge Balls

About 5 dozen candies

1/4 cup (1/2 stick) butter

1/2 cup REESE'S Creamy Peanut Butter

1/4 cup milk

3 2/3 cups powdered sugar

1 teaspoon vanilla extract

3 cups finely chopped peanuts

1 1/2 cups HERSHEY'S SPECIAL DARK Chocolate Chips or HERSHEY'S Semi-Sweet Chocolate Chips

1 1/2 teaspoons shortening (do not use butter, margarine, spread or oil)

1. Line 8- or 9-inch square pan with foil; butter foil.

2. Cook butter, peanut butter and milk in large saucepan over very low heat, stirring constantly, until mixture is melted. With wooden spoon gradually beat in powdered sugar and vanilla. Remove from heat; pour into prepared pan. Cool completely. (Mixture will appear dry, but softens when rolled into balls.)

3. Line two trays with wax paper. Spread chopped peanuts on one tray; set aside. Roll peanut butter mixture into 3/4-inch balls and place on second tray. If necessary, refrigerate peanut butter balls until firm enough to handle easily for coating.

4. Place chocolate chips and shortening in medium microwave-safe bowl. Microwave at MEDIUM (50%) 1 minute; stir. If necessary, microwave at MEDIUM an additional 15 seconds at a time, stirring after each heating, until chips are melted and mixture is smooth when stirred. Cool slightly.

5. Dip peanut butter balls completely into chocolate mixture, one at a time, with fork. Gently tap fork on side of bowl to remove excess chocolate. Immediately roll in chopped peanuts; gently reshape if necessary. Place candy balls into small paper candy cups or return to wax paper-lined tray. Refrigerate until firm, about 20 minutes. Store in cool, dry place.

NOTE Recipe can be doubled.

HERSHEY'S "Especially Dark" Chocolate Cake

Makes 10 to 12 servings

SPECIAL DARK DELIGHTS

2 cups sugar

1 3/4 cups all-purpose flour

3/4 cup HERSHEY'S SPECIAL DARK Cocoa

1 1/2 teaspoons baking powder

1 1/2 teaspoons baking soda

1 teaspoon salt

2 eggs

1 cup milk

1/2 cup vegetable oil

2 teaspoons vanilla extract

1 cup boiling water

"ESPECIALLY DARK" CHOCOLATE FROSTING (recipe follows)

1. Heat oven to 350°F. Grease and flour two 9-inch round baking pans.

2. Stir together sugar, flour, cocoa, baking powder, baking soda and salt in large bowl. Add eggs, milk, oil and vanilla; beat with electric mixer on medium speed for 2 minutes. Stir in boiling water (batter will be thin). Pour batter into prepared pans.

3. Bake 30 to 35 minutes or until wooden pick inserted in center comes out clean. Cool 10 minutes; remove from pans to wire racks. Cool completely. Frost with "ESPECIALLY DARK" CHOCOLATE FROSTING.

"Especially Dark" Chocolate Frosting

1/2 cup (1 stick) butter or margarine

2/3 cup HERSHEY'S SPECIAL DARK Cocoa

3 cups powdered sugar

1/3 cup milk

1 teaspoon vanilla extract

Melt butter. Stir in cocoa. Alternately add powdered sugar and milk, beating to spreading consistency. Add small amount additional milk, if needed. Stir in vanilla. Makes 2 cups frosting.

Fudgey Peanut Butter Chip Muffins

Makes 12 to 15 muffins

1/2	cup applesauce
1/2	cup quick-cooking rolled oats
1/4	cup (1/2 stick) butter or margarine, softened
1/2	cup granulated sugar
1/2	cup packed light brown sugar
1	egg
1/2	teaspoon vanilla extract
3/4	cup all-purpose flour
1/4	cup HERSHEY'S SPECIAL DARK Cocoa or HERSHEY'S Cocoa
1/2	teaspoon baking soda
1/4	teaspoon ground cinnamon (optional)
1	cup REESE'S Peanut Butter Chips
	Powdered sugar (optional)

1. Heat oven to 350°F. Line muffin cups (2 1/2 inches in diameter) with paper bake cups.

2. Stir together applesauce and oats in small bowl; set aside. Beat butter, granulated sugar, brown sugar, egg and vanilla in large bowl until well blended. Add applesauce mixture; blend well. Stir together flour, cocoa, baking soda and cinnamon, if desired. Add to butter mixture, blending well. Stir in peanut butter chips. Fill muffin cups 3/4 full with batter.

3. Bake 22 to 26 minutes or until wooden pick inserted in center comes out almost clean. Cool slightly in pan on wire rack. Sprinkle muffin tops with powdered sugar, if desired. Serve warm.

FUDGEY CHOCOLATE CHIP MUFFINS: Omit Peanut Butter Chips. Add 1 cup HERSHEY'S SPECIAL DARK Chocolate Chips or HERSHEY'S Semi-Sweet Chocolate Chips.

IMPRESSIVE
Cakes & Cheesecakes

Chocolate Cake Fingers

Makes 42 pieces

1 cup sugar

1 cup all-purpose flour

1/3 cup HERSHEY'S Cocoa

3/4 teaspoon baking powder

3/4 teaspoon baking soda

1/2 cup nonfat milk

1/4 cup frozen egg substitute, thawed

1/4 cup canola oil or vegetable oil

1 teaspoon vanilla extract

1/2 cup boiling water

Powdered sugar

1 teaspoon freshly grated orange peel

1 1/2 cups frozen light non-dairy whipped topping, thawed

1. Heat oven to 350°F. Line bottom of 13×9×2-inch baking pan with wax paper.

2. Stir together sugar, flour, cocoa, baking powder and baking soda in large bowl. Add milk, egg substitute, oil and vanilla; beat on medium speed of mixer 2 minutes. Stir in boiling water (batter will be thin). Pour into prepared pan.

3. Bake 16 to 18 minutes or until wooden pick inserted in center comes out clean. With knife or metal spatula, loosen cake from edges of pan. Place clean, lint-free dish towel on wire rack; sprinkle lightly with powdered sugar. Invert cake on towel; peel off wax paper. Cool completely.

4. Invert cake, right side up, on cutting board. Cut cake into small rectangles (about 2×1 1/4 inches). Stir orange peel into whipped topping; spoon dollop on each piece of cake. Garnish as desired. Store ungarnished cake, covered, at room temperature.

Strawberry Chocolate Chip Shortcake

Makes 12 servings

1 cup sugar, divided

$1/2$ cup (1 stick) butter or margarine, softened

1 egg

2 teaspoons vanilla extract, divided

$1 1/2$ cups all-purpose flour

$1/2$ teaspoon baking powder

1 cup HERSHEY'S Mini Chips Semi-Sweet Chocolate, HERSHEY'S SPECIAL DARK Chocolate Chips or HERSHEY'S Semi-Sweet Chocolate Chips, divided

1 container (16 ounces) dairy sour cream

2 eggs

2 cups frozen non-dairy whipped topping, thawed

Fresh strawberries, rinsed and halved

1. Heat oven to 350°F. Grease 9-inch springform pan.

2. Beat $1/2$ cup sugar and butter in large bowl. Add 1 egg and 1 teaspoon vanilla; beat until creamy. Gradually add flour and baking powder, beating until smooth; stir in $1/2$ cup small chocolate chips. Press mixture onto bottom of prepared pan.

3. Stir together sour cream, remaining $1/2$ cup sugar, 2 eggs and remaining 1 teaspoon vanilla in medium bowl; stir in remaining $1/2$ cup small chocolate chips. Pour over mixture in pan.

4. Bake 50 to 55 minutes until almost set in center and edges are lightly browned. Cool completely on wire rack; remove side of pan. Spread whipped topping over top. Cover; refrigerate. Just before serving, arrange strawberry halves on top of cake; garnish as desired. Refrigerate leftover dessert.

Orange Streusel Coffeecake

Makes 12 servings

COCOA STREUSEL
(recipe follows)

3/4 cup (1 1/2 sticks) butter or margarine, softened

1 cup sugar

3 eggs

1 teaspoon vanilla extract

1/2 cup dairy sour cream

3 cups all-purpose flour

2 teaspoons baking powder

1 teaspoon baking soda

1 cup orange juice

2 teaspoons grated orange peel

1/2 cup orange marmalade or apple jelly

1. Prepare COCOA STREUSEL. Heat oven to 350°F. Generously grease 12-cup fluted tube pan.

2. Beat butter and sugar in large bowl until well blended. Add eggs and vanilla; beat well. Add sour cream; beat until blended. Stir together flour, baking powder and baking soda; add alternately with orange juice to butter mixture, beating until well blended. Stir in orange peel.

3. Spread marmalade in bottom of prepared pan; sprinkle half of streusel over marmalade. Pour half of batter into pan, spreading evenly. Sprinkle remaining streusel over batter; spread remaining batter evenly over streusel.

4. Bake about 1 hour or until wooden pick inserted near center of cake comes out clean. Loosen cake from side of pan with metal spatula; immediately invert onto serving plate. Serve warm or cool.

COCOA STREUSEL: Stir together 2/3 cup packed light brown sugar, 1/2 cup chopped walnuts, 1/4 cup HERSHEY'S Cocoa and 1/2 cup MOUNDS Sweetened Coconut Flakes, if desired.

CAKES & CHEESECAKES

106

Three Layer Cheesecake Squares

Makes 9 to 12 servings

CHOCOLATE CRUMB
CRUST (recipe follows)

3 packages (8 ounces each)
cream cheese, softened

3/4 cup sugar

3 eggs

1/3 cup dairy sour cream

3 tablespoons all-purpose
flour

1 teaspoon vanilla extract

1 cup REESE'S Peanut
Butter Chips, melted

1 cup HERSHEY'S SPECIAL
DARK Chocolate Chips or
HERSHEY'S Semi-Sweet
Chocolate Chips, melted

1 cup HERSHEY'S Premier
White Chips, melted

THREE LAYER DRIZZLE
(recipe follows)

1. Heat oven to 350°F. Line 9-inch square baking pan with foil, extending edges over pan sides; grease lightly. Prepare CHOCOLATE CRUMB CRUST.

2. Beat cream cheese and sugar until smooth. Gradually add eggs, sour cream, flour and vanilla; beat well. Stir 1 1/3 cups batter into melted peanut butter chips; pour over prepared crust. Stir 1 1/3 cups batter into melted chocolate chips; carefully spoon over peanut butter layer. Stir remaining batter into melted white chips; carefully spoon over chocolate layer.

3. Bake 40 to 45 minutes or until almost set. Cool completely on wire rack.

4. Prepare THREE LAYER DRIZZLE. Drizzle, one flavor at a time, over cheesecake. Refrigerate about 3 hours or until drizzle is firm. Use foil to lift cheesecake out of pan; cut into squares. Garnish as desired. Cover; refrigerate leftover cheesecake.

CHOCOLATE CRUMB CRUST: Heat conventional oven to 350°F. Combine 1 1/2 cups (about 45 wafers) vanilla wafer crumbs, 6 tablespoons powdered sugar, 6 tablespoons HERSHEY'S Cocoa and 6 tablespoons melted butter or margarine. Press onto bottom of prepared pan. Bake 8 minutes; cool slightly.

THREE LAYER DRIZZLE: Melt 1 tablespoon REESE'S Peanut Butter Chips with 1/2 teaspoon shortening, stirring until chips are melted and mixture is smooth. Repeat with 1 tablespoon HERSHEY'S SPECIAL DARK Chocolate Chips or HERSHEY'S Semi-Sweet Chocolate Chips with 1/2 teaspoon shortening and 1 tablespoon HERSHEY'S Premier White Chips with 1/2 teaspoon shortening.

Chocolate Syrup Swirl Cake

Makes 20 servings

1 cup (2 sticks) butter or margarine, softened

2 cups sugar

2 teaspoons vanilla extract

3 eggs

2 3/4 cups all-purpose flour

1 1/4 teaspoons baking soda, divided

1/2 teaspoon salt

1 cup buttermilk or sour milk*

1 cup HERSHEY'S Syrup

1 cup MOUNDS Sweetened Coconut Flakes (optional)

*To sour milk:
Use 1 tablespoon white vinegar plus milk to equal 1 cup.

1. Heat oven to 350°F. Grease and flour 12-cup fluted tube pan or 10-inch tube pan.

2. Beat butter, sugar and vanilla in large bowl until fluffy. Add eggs; beat well. Stir together flour, 1 teaspoon baking soda and salt; add alternately with buttermilk to butter mixture, beating until well blended.

3. Measure 2 cups batter in small bowl; stir in syrup and remaining 1/4 teaspoon baking soda. Add coconut, if desired, to remaining vanilla batter; pour into prepared pan. Pour chocolate batter over vanilla batter in pan; do not mix.

4. Bake 60 to 70 minutes or until wooden pick inserted in center comes out clean. Cool 15 minutes; remove from pan to wire rack. Cool completely; glaze or frost as desired.

Chilled Raspberry Cheesecake

Makes 10 to 12 servings

1 1/2 cups vanilla wafer crumbs (about 45 wafers, crushed)

1/3 cup HERSHEY'S Cocoa

1/3 cup powdered sugar

1/3 cup butter or margarine, melted

1 package (10 ounces) frozen raspberries, thawed

1 envelope unflavored gelatin

1/2 cup cold water

1/2 cup boiling water

2 packages (8 ounces each) cream cheese, softened

1/2 cup granulated sugar

1 teaspoon vanilla extract

3 tablespoons seedless red raspberry preserves

CHOCOLATE WHIPPED CREAM (recipe follows)

1. Heat oven to 350°F.

2. Stir together crumbs, 1/3 cup cocoa and 1/3 cup powdered sugar in medium bowl; stir in melted butter. Press mixture onto bottom and 1 1/2 inches up side of 9-inch springform pan. Bake 10 minutes; cool completely.

3. Purée and strain raspberries; set aside. Sprinkle gelatin over cold water in small bowl; let stand several minutes to soften. Add boiling water; stir until gelatin dissolves completely and mixture is clear. Beat cream cheese, granulated sugar and 1 teaspoon vanilla in large bowl until smooth. Gradually add raspberry purée and gelatin, mixing thoroughly; pour into prepared crust.

4. Refrigerate several hours or overnight. Loosen cake from side of pan with knife; remove side of pan. Spread raspberry preserves over top. Garnish with CHOCOLATE WHIPPED CREAM. Cover; refrigerate leftovers.

CHOCOLATE WHIPPED CREAM: Stir together 1/2 cup powdered sugar and 1/4 cup HERSHEY'S Cocoa in medium bowl. Add 1 cup cold whipping cream and 1 teaspoon vanilla extract; beat until stiff.

Peanut Butter Coffeecake

Makes 12 to 15 servings

1²/₃ cups (10-ounce package) REESE'S Peanut Butter Chips

³/₄ cup REESE'S Creamy Peanut Butter

2¹/₄ cups all-purpose flour

1¹/₂ cups packed light brown sugar

¹/₂ cup (1 stick) butter or margarine, softened

1 teaspoon baking powder

¹/₂ teaspoon baking soda

1 cup milk

3 eggs

1 teaspoon vanilla extract

1. Heat oven to 350°F. Grease bottom of 13×9×2-inch baking pan.

2. Place peanut butter chips and peanut butter in microwave-safe bowl. Microwave at MEDIUM (50%) 1 minute; stir. If necessary, microwave at MEDIUM an additional 15 seconds at a time, stirring after each heating, just until chips are melted when stirred.

3. Combine flour, brown sugar, butter and peanut butter chip mixture in large bowl. Beat on low speed of mixer until mixture resembles small crumbs; reserve 1 cup crumbs. To remaining crumb mixture, gradually blend in baking powder, baking soda, milk, eggs and vanilla; beat until well combined. Pour batter into prepared pan; sprinkle with reserved crumbs.

4. Bake 35 to 40 minutes or until wooden pick inserted in center comes out clean. Cool completely in pan on wire rack.

Brickle Bundt Cake

Makes 12 to 14 servings

$1^1/3$ cups (8-ounce package) HEATH BITS 'O BRICKLE Toffee Bits, divided

$1^1/4$ cups granulated sugar, divided

$1/4$ cup chopped walnuts

1 teaspoon ground cinnamon

$1/2$ cup (1 stick) butter, softened

2 eggs

$1^1/4$ teaspoons vanilla extract, divided

2 cups all-purpose flour

$1^1/2$ teaspoons baking powder

1 teaspoon baking soda

$1/4$ teaspoon salt

1 container (8 ounces) dairy sour cream

$1/4$ cup ($1/2$ stick) butter, melted

1 cup powdered sugar

1 to 3 tablespoons milk, divided

1. Heat oven to 325°F. Grease and flour 12-cup fluted tube pan or 10-inch tube pan. Set aside $1/4$ cup toffee bits for topping. Combine remaining toffee bits, $1/4$ cup granulated sugar, walnuts and cinnamon; set aside.

2. Beat remaining 1 cup granulated sugar and $1/2$ cup butter in large bowl until fluffy. Add eggs and 1 teaspoon vanilla; beat well. Stir together flour, baking powder, baking soda and salt; gradually add to butter mixture alternately with sour cream, beating until blended. Beat 3 minutes. Spoon one-third of the batter into prepared pan. Sprinkle with half of toffee mixture. Spoon half of remaining batter into pan. Top with remaining toffee mixture. Spoon remaining batter into pan. Pour melted butter over batter.

3. Bake 45 to 50 minutes or until wooden pick inserted in center comes out clean. Cool 10 minutes; remove from pan to wire rack. Cool completely.

4. Stir together powdered sugar, 1 tablespoon milk and remaining $1/4$ teaspoon vanilla. Stir in additional milk, 1 teaspoon at a time, until desired consistency; drizzle over cake. Sprinkle with reserved $1/4$ cup toffee bits.

Chocolate & Peanut Butter Fudge Cheesecake

Makes 10 to 12 servings

1 1/2 cups vanilla wafer crumbs (about 45 wafers, crushed)

1/2 cup powdered sugar

1/4 cup HERSHEY'S Cocoa

1/3 cup butter or margarine, melted

3 packages (8 ounces each) cream cheese, softened

3/4 cup granulated sugar

3 eggs

1/3 cup dairy sour cream

3 tablespoons all-purpose flour

1 teaspoon vanilla extract

1/4 teaspoon salt

1 cup HERSHEY'S SPECIAL DARK Chocolate Chips or HERSHEY'S Semi-Sweet Chocolate Chips, melted

1 cup REESE'S Peanut Butter Chips, melted

HERSHEY'S Fudge Topping (optional)

Sweetened whipped cream (optional)

1. Heat oven to 350°F. Combine vanilla wafer crumbs, powdered sugar, cocoa and melted butter in medium bowl. Press onto bottom and 1 inch up side of 9-inch springform pan. Bake 8 minutes; cool.

2. Beat cream cheese and granulated sugar in large bowl until smooth. Add eggs, sour cream, flour, vanilla and salt; beat until well blended.

3. Place half of batter in separate bowl. Stir melted chocolate into one bowl of cream cheese mixture and melted peanut butter chips into the other. Spread chocolate mixture in prepared crust. Gently spread peanut butter mixture over chocolate mixture. Do not stir.

4. Bake 50 to 55 minutes or until center is almost set. (For less cracking of cheesecake surface, bake in water bath.) Remove from oven to wire rack. With knife, loosen cake from side of pan. Cool completely; remove side of pan. Cover; refrigerate.

5. To serve, drizzle each slice with fudge topping and top with whipped cream, if desired. Cover; refrigerate leftover cheesecake.

Cinnamon Chip Applesauce Coffeecake

Makes 12 to 15 servings

1	cup (2 sticks) butter or margarine, softened
1	cup granulated sugar
2	eggs
1/2	teaspoon vanilla extract
3/4	cup applesauce
2 1/2	cups all-purpose flour
1	teaspoon baking soda
1/2	teaspoon salt
1 2/3	cups (10-ounce package) HERSHEY'S Cinnamon Chips
1	cup chopped pecans (optional)
3/4	cup powdered sugar
1	to 2 tablespoons warm water

1. Heat oven to 350°F. Lightly grease 13×9×2-inch baking pan.

2. Beat butter and granulated sugar with electric mixer on medium speed in large bowl until well blended. Beat in eggs and vanilla. Mix in applesauce. Stir together flour, baking soda and salt; gradually add to butter mixture, beating until well blended. Stir in cinnamon chips and pecans, if desired. Spread in prepared pan.

3. Bake 30 to 35 minutes or until wooden pick inserted in center comes out clean. Cool in pan on wire rack. Sprinkle cake with powdered sugar or stir together 3/4 cup powdered sugar and warm water to make smooth glaze; drizzle over cake. Serve at room temperature or while still slightly warm.

FLUTED CAKE: Grease and flour 12-cup fluted tube pan. Prepare batter as directed; pour into prepared pan. Bake 45 to 50 minutes or until wooden pick inserted in thickest part comes out clean. Cool 15 minutes; invert onto wire rack. Cool completely.

CUPCAKES: Line 24 baking cups (2 1/2 inches in diameter) with paper baking liners. Prepare batter as directed; divide evenly into prepared cups. Bake 15 to 18 minutes or until wooden pick inserted in center comes out clean. Cool completely.

CAKES & CHEESECAKES

Fiesta Fantasy Cake

Makes 16 to 20 servings

2 cups sifted cake flour or 1³/₄ cups sifted all-purpose flour

¹/₂ cup HERSHEY'S SPECIAL DARK Cocoa or HERSHEY'S Cocoa

2 teaspoons baking soda

¹/₄ teaspoon salt

2 cups packed light brown sugar

²/₃ cup butter, softened

3 eggs

1 tablespoon coffee liqueur or strong coffee

¹/₂ teaspoon vanilla extract

1 container (8 ounces) dairy sour cream

³/₄ cup boiling water

CHOCOLATE MOUSSE (recipe follows)

CHOCOLATE FROSTING (recipe follows)

1. Heat oven to 350°F. Grease and flour two 9-inch round cake pans. Combine flour, cocoa, baking soda and salt. Set aside.

2. Beat brown sugar and butter with electric mixer on low or medium speed in large bowl until combined. Add eggs, one at a time, beating well after each addition. Beat in coffee liqueur or coffee and vanilla. Add flour mixture and sour cream alternately to sugar mixture, beating after each addition just until combined. Stir in boiling water until blended. Pour into prepared pans.

3. Bake 30 to 35 minutes or until wooden pick inserted near centers comes out clean. Cool in pans on wire racks 10 minutes; remove from pans to wire racks. Cool completely.

4. Prepare CHOCOLATE MOUSSE. Split each cake layer horizontally to make four layers total. Place one layer on serving plate; spread with one-third (about 1 cup) CHOCOLATE MOUSSE. Repeat layering with two of the remaining layers and remaining mousse. Place remaining cake layer on top. Prepare CHOCOLATE FROSTING; frost cake top and sides. Cover; refrigerate at least 2 hours before serving.

Chocolate Mousse

2 cups (12-ounce package) HERSHEY'S SPECIAL DARK Chocolate Chips or HERSHEY'S Semi-Sweet Chocolate Chips

1¹/₃ cups whipping cream, divided

3 tablespoons sugar

¹/₄ cup coffee liqueur or strong coffee

1 tablespoon vanilla extract

Place chocolate chips in food processor bowl; process until finely ground. Mix ¹/₃ cup whipping cream and sugar in

1-quart saucepan. Cook over medium heat, stirring constantly, until sugar is dissolved and mixture is just boiling. With food processor running, pour hot cream through feed tube, processing 10 to 20 seconds or until chocolate is completely melted. Scrape side of food processor bowl. Add liqueur or strong coffee and vanilla extract; process 10 to 20 seconds or until smooth. Pour into large bowl; cool about 10 minutes or until mixture is room temperature. Beat remaining 1 cup whipping cream in chilled medium bowl with electric mixer on high speed just until soft peaks form. Fold whipped cream into chocolate mixture. Cover; refrigerate at least 30 minutes.

Chocolate Frosting

$1^1/_2$ cups sifted powdered sugar

$^2/_3$ cup HERSHEY'S SPECIAL DARK Cocoa

$1^1/_2$ cups whipping cream

1 teaspoon vanilla extract

3 to 4 tablespoons milk

Stir together powdered sugar and cocoa in medium mixer bowl. Stir in whipping cream and vanilla. Beat on low speed of mixer until stiff peaks form, scraping side of bowl constantly. (Mixture will be very stiff.) By hand, stir in milk 1 tablespoon at a time to make desired consistency.

Rich HEATH Bits Cheesecake

Makes 12 to 16 servings

VANILLA WAFER CRUST
(recipe follows)

3 packages (8 ounces each)
   cream cheese, softened

1 cup sugar

3 eggs

1 container (8 ounces)
   sour cream

$^1/_2$ teaspoon vanilla extract

$1^1/_3$ cups (8-ounce package)
   HEATH Milk Chocolate
   Toffee Bits, divided

1. Prepare VANILLA WAFER CRUST. Heat oven to 350°F.

2. Beat cream cheese and sugar in large bowl on medium speed of mixer until well blended. Add eggs, one at a time, beating well after each addition. Add sour cream and vanilla; beat on low speed until blended.

3. Pour half of cheese mixture into crust. Reserve $^1/_4$ cup toffee bits for topping; sprinkle remaining toffee bits over cheese mixture in pan. Spoon in remaining cheese mixture.

4. Bake 1 hour or until filling is set. Cool 15 minutes. Sprinkle reserved toffee bits over top; with knife, loosen cake from side of pan. Cool completely; remove side of pan. Cover, refrigerate at least 4 hours before serving. Cover; refrigerate leftover cheesecake.

VANILLA WAFER CRUST: Combine $1^3/_4$ cups vanilla wafer crumbs (about 55 wafers) and 2 tablespoons sugar; stir in $^1/_4$ cup ($^1/_2$ stick) melted butter or margarine. Press onto bottom and 1 inch up side of 9-inch springform pan. Refrigerate about 30 minutes.

Spicy Butterscotch Snack Cake

Makes 12 to 16 servings

1	cup (2 sticks) butter or margarine, softened
1	cup sugar
2	eggs
1/2	teaspoon vanilla extract
1/2	cup applesauce
2 1/2	cups all-purpose flour
1 1/2	to 2 teaspoons ground cinnamon
1	teaspoon baking soda
1/2	teaspoon salt
1 3/4	cups (11-ounce package) HERSHEY'S Butterscotch Chips
1	cup chopped pecans (optional)
	Powdered sugar or frozen whipped topping, thawed (optional)

1. Heat oven to 350°F. Lightly grease 13×9×2-inch baking pan.

2. Beat butter and sugar in large bowl until fluffy. Add eggs and vanilla; beat well. Mix in applesauce. Stir together flour, cinnamon, baking soda and salt; gradually add to butter mixture, beating until well blended. Stir in butterscotch chips and pecans, if desired. Spread in prepared pan.

3. Bake 35 to 40 minutes or until wooden pick inserted in center comes out clean. Cool completely in pan. Dust with powdered sugar or serve with whipped topping, if desired.

FESTIVE FAVORITES FOR
Special Occasions

Cherry-Glazed Chocolate Torte
Makes 10 to 12 servings

1/2 cup (1 stick) butter or margarine, melted

1 cup granulated sugar

1 teaspoon vanilla extract

2 eggs

1/2 cup all-purpose flour

1/3 cup HERSHEY'S Cocoa

1/4 teaspoon baking powder

1/4 teaspoon salt

1 package (8 ounces) cream cheese, softened

1 cup powdered sugar

1 cup frozen non-dairy whipped topping, thawed

1 can (21 ounces) cherry pie filling, divided

1. Heat oven to 350°F. Grease bottom of 9-inch springform pan.

2. Stir together butter, granulated sugar and vanilla in large bowl. Add eggs; using spoon, beat well. Stir together flour, cocoa, baking powder and salt; gradually add to egg mixture, beating until well blended. Spread batter in prepared pan.

3. Bake 25 to 30 minutes or until cake is set. (Cake will be fudgey and will not test done.) Remove from oven; cool completely in pan on wire rack.

4. Beat cream cheese and powdered sugar in medium bowl until well blended; gradually fold in whipped topping, blending well. Spread over top of cake. Spread 1 cup cherry pie filling over cream layer; refrigerate several hours. With knife, loosen cake from side of pan; remove side of pan. Cut into wedges; garnish with remaining pie filling. Cover; refrigerate leftover dessert.

Chocolate Buttercream Cherry Candies

Makes about 48 candies

About 48 maraschino cherries with stems, well drained

1/4 cup (1/2 stick) butter, softened

2 cups powdered sugar

1/4 cup HERSHEY'S Cocoa or HERSHEY'S SPECIAL DARK Cocoa

1 to 2 tablespoons milk, divided

1/2 teaspoon vanilla extract

1/4 teaspoon almond extract

WHITE CHIP COATING (recipe follows)

CHOCOLATE CHIP DRIZZLE (recipe follows)

1. Cover tray with wax paper. Lightly press cherries between layers of paper towels to remove excess moisture.

2. Beat butter, powdered sugar, cocoa and 1 tablespoon milk in small bowl until well blended; stir in vanilla and almond extract. If necessary, add remaining milk, one teaspoon at a time, until mixture will hold together but is not wet.

3. Mold scant teaspoon mixture around each cherry, covering completely; place on prepared tray. Cover; refrigerate 3 hours or until firm.

4. Prepare WHITE CHIP COATING. Holding each cherry by stem, dip into coating. Place on tray; refrigerate until firm.

5. About 1 hour before serving, prepare CHOCOLATE CHIP DRIZZLE; with tines of fork drizzle randomly over candies. Refrigerate until drizzle is firm. Store in refrigerator.

WHITE CHIP COATING: Place 2 cups (12-ounce package) HERSHEY'S Premier White Chips in small microwave-safe bowl; drizzle with 2 tablespoons vegetable oil. Microwave at MEDIUM (50%) 1 minute; stir. If necessary, microwave at MEDIUM an additional 15 seconds at a time, stirring after each heating just until chips are melted and mixture is smooth. If mixture thickens while coating, microwave at MEDIUM 15 seconds; stir until smooth.

CHOCOLATE CHIP DRIZZLE: Place 1/4 cup HERSHEY'S Semi-Sweet Chocolate Chips and 1/4 teaspoon shortening (do not use butter, margarine, spread or oil) in another small microwave-safe bowl. Microwave at MEDIUM (50%) 30 seconds to 1 minute; stir until chips are melted and mixture is smooth.

Chocolate Raspberry Dessert

Makes about 12 servings

1 cup all-purpose flour

1 cup sugar

1/2 cup (1 stick) butter or margarine, softened

1/4 teaspoon baking powder

4 eggs

1 1/2 cups (16-ounce can) HERSHEY'S Syrup

RASPBERRY CREAM CENTER (recipe follows)

CHOCOLATE GLAZE (recipe follows)

1. Heat oven to 350°F. Grease 13×9×2-inch baking pan.

2. Combine flour, sugar, butter, baking powder and eggs in large bowl; beat until smooth. Add syrup; blend thoroughly. Pour batter into prepared pan.

3. Bake 25 to 30 minutes or until wooden pick inserted in center comes out clean. Cool completely in pan on wire rack. Spread RASPBERRY CREAM CENTER on cake. Cover; refrigerate. Pour CHOCOLATE GLAZE over chilled dessert. Cover; refrigerate at least 1 hour before serving. Cover; refrigerate leftover dessert.

RASPBERRY CREAM CENTER: Combine 2 cups powdered sugar, 1/2 cup (1 stick) softened butter or margarine and 2 tablespoons raspberry-flavored liqueur* in small bowl; beat until smooth. (A few drops red food coloring may be added, if desired.)

*1/4 cup raspberry preserves mixed with 1 teaspoon water may be substituted for the raspberry-flavored liqueur.

CHOCOLATE GLAZE: Melt 6 tablespoons butter or margarine and 1 cup HERSHEY'S SPECIAL DARK Chocolate Chips or HERSHEY'S Semi-Sweet Chocolate Chips in small saucepan over very low heat. Remove from heat; stir until smooth. Cool slightly.

Hot Chocolate Soufflé

Makes 8 to 10 servings

1 cup HERSHEY'S Cocoa

1 1/4 cups sugar, divided

1/2 cup all-purpose flour

1/4 teaspoon salt

2 cups milk

6 egg yolks, well beaten

2 tablespoons butter or margarine

1 teaspoon vanilla extract

8 egg whites

1/4 teaspoon cream of tartar

Sweetened whipped cream

1. Move oven rack to lowest position. Heat oven to 350°F. Lightly butter 2 1/2-quart soufflé dish; sprinkle with sugar. For collar, cut a length of heavy-duty aluminum foil to fit around soufflé dish; fold in thirds lengthwise. Lightly butter one side of foil. Attach foil, buttered side in, around outside of dish, allowing foil to extend at least 2 inches above dish. Secure foil with tape or string.

2. Stir together cocoa, 1 cup sugar, flour and salt in large saucepan; gradually stir in milk. Cook over medium heat, stirring constantly with wire whisk, until mixture boils; remove from heat. Gradually stir small amount of chocolate mixture into beaten egg yolks; blend well. Add egg mixture to chocolate mixture in pan, blending well. Cook and stir 1 minute. Add butter and vanilla, stirring until blended. Set aside; cool 20 minutes.

3. Beat egg whites with cream of tartar in large bowl until soft peaks form; gradually add remaining 1/4 cup sugar, beating until stiff peaks form. Gently fold about one-third of beaten egg white mixture into chocolate mixture. Lightly fold chocolate mixture, half at a time, into remaining beaten egg white mixture just until blended; do not overfold.

4. Gently pour mixture into prepared dish; smooth top with spatula. Gently place dish in larger baking pan; pour hot water into larger pan to depth of 1 inch.

5. Bake 1 hour and 5 to 10 minutes or until puffed and set. Remove soufflé dish from water. Carefully remove foil. Serve immediately with sweetened whipped cream.

132

Chocolate Mini-Puffs

Makes about 2 to 2½ dozen mini-puffs

½ cup water

¼ cup (½ stick) butter or margarine

⅛ teaspoon salt

½ cup all-purpose flour

2 eggs

CHOCOLATE MOUSSE FILLING (recipe follows)

CHOCOLATE GLAZE (recipe follows) or powdered sugar

1. Heat oven to 400°F.

2. Combine water, butter and salt in medium saucepan. Cook over medium heat, stirring constantly, until mixture comes to full rolling boil; turn heat to low.

3. Add flour all at once; cook over low heat, stirring vigorously, until mixture leaves side of pan and forms a ball, about 1 minute. Remove from heat; cool slightly. Add eggs, one at a time, beating with wooden spoon until smooth and velvety. Drop by scant teaspoonfuls onto ungreased cookie sheet.

4. Bake 25 to 30 minutes or until puffed and golden brown. Remove from oven; cool on wire rack.

5. Prepare CHOCOLATE MOUSSE FILLING. Slice off tops of puffs. With spoon, fill puffs with filling or pipe filling into puffs using a pastry bag fitted with ¼-inch tip. Replace tops and sprinkle with powdered sugar or prepare CHOCOLATE GLAZE; drizzle onto puffs. Refrigerate until serving time. Cover; refrigerate leftover puffs.

Chocolate Mousse Filling

1 teaspoon unflavored gelatin

1 tablespoon cold water

2 tablespoons boiling water

½ cup sugar

¼ cup HERSHEY'S Cocoa

1 cup (½ pint) cold whipping cream

1 teaspoon vanilla extract

1. Sprinkle gelatin over cold water in small bowl; let stand 1 minute to soften. Add boiling water; stir until gelatin is completely dissolved and mixture is clear. Cool slightly.

2. Stir together sugar and cocoa in medium bowl; add whipping cream and vanilla. Beat at medium speed, scraping bottom of bowl occasionally, until stiff; pour in gelatin mixture and beat until well blended. Refrigerate 1/2 hour. Makes about 2 cups filling.

CHOCOLATE GLAZE:

1. Melt 2 tablespoons butter or margarine in small saucepan over low heat; add 2 tablespoons HERSHEY'S Cocoa and 2 tablespoons water. Cook and stir over low heat until smooth and slightly thickened; do not boil. Remove from heat; cool slightly.

2. Gradually add in 1 cup powdered sugar and 1/2 teaspoon vanilla extract, beating to desired consistency.

Chocolate and Orange Meltaways

About 2 dozen pieces

2 cups (12-ounce package) HERSHEY'S Premier White Chips

1/2 cup (1 stick) unsalted butter (do not substitute margarine)

1/3 cup whipping cream

1 1/2 teaspoons orange extract

CHOCOLATE COATING (recipe follows)

1/2 teaspoon shortening (do not use butter, margarine, spread or oil)

1. Line tray with wax paper. Reserve 2 tablespoons white chips.

2. Combine butter and whipping cream in medium saucepan; cook over low heat, stirring constantly until mixture comes to a full rolling boil. Remove from heat; immediately add remaining white chips. Stir with whisk until smooth. Add orange extract; blend well.

3. Refrigerate until firm enough to handle, about 2 hours. Taking small amount of mixture at a time, shape into 1-inch balls. Place on prepared tray; refrigerate until firm, about 1 1/2 hours. Prepare CHOCOLATE COATING. Place one candy onto fork; dip into coating, covering completely and allowing excess to drip off. Place candies onto prepared tray. Repeat with remaining candies. Refrigerate until coating is set, about 1 hour.

4. Place reserved 2 tablespoons white chips and shortening in small microwave-safe bowl. Microwave at MEDIUM (50%) 30 seconds; stir. If necessary, microwave at MEDIUM an additional 10 seconds or until mixture is smooth when stirred. With fork, lightly drizzle over coated candies; refrigerate until set, about 20 minutes. Cover; store in refrigerator.

CHOCOLATE COATING: Place 2 packages (4 ounces each) HERSHEY'S SPECIAL DARK Chocolate Premium Baking Bar, broken into pieces and 1 teaspoon shortening (do not use butter, margarine, spread or oil) in medium microwave-safe bowl. Microwave at MEDIUM 2 minutes; stir. If necessary, microwave at MEDIUM an additional 15 seconds at a time, stirring after each heating, until chocolate is melted and mixture is smooth when stirred. Cool slightly. (If chocolate is too hot, it will not coat candy.)

Holiday Chocolate Cake

Makes 10 to 12 servings

2 cups sugar

1 3/4 cups all-purpose flour

3/4 cup HERSHEY'S Cocoa

2 teaspoons baking soda

1 teaspoon baking powder

1 teaspoon salt

1 cup buttermilk or sour milk*

1 cup strong black coffee or 2 teaspoons instant coffee dissolved in 1 cup hot water

1/2 cup vegetable oil

2 eggs

2 teaspoons vanilla extract

RICOTTA CHEESE FILLING (recipe follows)

CHOCOLATE WHIPPED CREAM (recipe follows)

VANILLA WHIPPED CREAM (recipe follows)

Candied red or green cherries (optional)

*To sour milk:
Use 1 tablespoon white vinegar plus milk to equal 1 cup.

1. Heat oven to 350°F. Grease and flour two 9-inch round baking pans.

2. Stir together sugar, flour, cocoa, baking soda, baking powder and salt in large bowl. Add buttermilk, coffee, oil, eggs and vanilla; beat at medium speed of mixer 2 minutes (batter will be thin). Pour batter into prepared pans.

3. Bake 30 to 35 minutes or until wooden pick inserted into center of cakes comes out clean. Cool 10 minutes; remove from pans to wire racks. Cool completely.

4. Slice cake layers in half horizontally. Place bottom slice on serving plate; top with 1/3 RICOTTA CHEESE FILLING. Alternate cake layers and filling, ending with cake on top. Frost cake with CHOCOLATE WHIPPED CREAM. Decorate with VANILLA WHIPPED CREAM and cherries, if desired. Cover; refrigerate leftover cake.

Ricotta Cheese Filling

1 3/4 cups (15 ounces) ricotta cheese*

1/4 cup sugar

3 tablespoons GRAND MARNIER (orange-flavored liqueur) or orange juice concentrate, undiluted

1/4 cup candied red or green cherries, coarsely chopped

1/3 cup HERSHEY'S Mini Chips Semi-Sweet Chocolate

*1 cup (1/2 pint) whipping cream can be substituted for ricotta cheese. Beat with sugar and liqueur until stiff. Fold in candied cherries and small chocolate chips.

Beat ricotta cheese, sugar and liqueur in large bowl until smooth. Fold in candied cherries and small chocolate chips.

CHOCOLATE WHIPPED CREAM: Stir together 1/3 cup powdered sugar and 2 tablespoons HERSHEY'S Cocoa in small bowl. Add 1 cup (1/2 pint) cold whipping cream and 1 teaspoon vanilla extract; beat until stiff.

VANILLA WHIPPED CREAM: Beat 1/2 cup cold whipping cream, 2 tablespoons powdered sugar and 1/2 teaspoon vanilla extract in small bowl until stiff.

White Chip Fruit Tart

Makes 10 to 12 servings

3/4 cup (1 1/2 sticks) butter or margarine, softened

1/2 cup powdered sugar

1 1/2 cups all-purpose flour

2 cups (12-ounce package) HERSHEY'S Premier White Chips

1/4 cup whipping cream

1 package (8 ounces) cream cheese, softened

FRUIT TOPPING (recipe follows)

Assorted fresh fruit, sliced

1. Heat oven to 300°F.

2. Beat butter and powdered sugar in small bowl until smooth; blend in flour. Press mixture onto bottom and up side of 12-inch round pizza pan. Flute edge, if desired.

3. Bake 20 to 25 minutes or until lightly browned; cool completely.

4. Place white chips and whipping cream in medium microwave-safe bowl. Microwave at MEDIUM (50%) 1 to 1 1/2 minutes or until chips are melted and mixture is smooth when stirred. Beat in cream cheese. Spread on cooled crust. Prepare FRUIT TOPPING. Arrange fruit over chip mixture; carefully pour or brush topping over fruit. Cover; refrigerate assembled tart until just before serving.

Fruit Topping

1/4 cup sugar

1 tablespoon cornstarch

1/2 cup pineapple juice

1/2 teaspoon lemon juice

Stir together sugar and cornstarch in small saucepan; stir in juices. Cook over medium heat, stirring constantly, until thickened; cool.

Chocolate Cups with Lemon Cream

Makes about 6 filled cups

1/2 cup sugar

1/4 cup plus 2 tablespoons all-purpose flour

2 tablespoons HERSHEY'S Cocoa

2 egg whites

1/4 cup (1/2 stick) butter or margarine, melted

CHOCOLATE COATING (recipe follows)

LEMON CREAM (recipe follows)

Freshly shredded lemon peel (optional)

1. Heat oven to 400°F. Grease and flour cookie sheet.

2. Stir together sugar, flour and cocoa in small bowl. Add egg whites and butter; beat until smooth. Drop teaspoonfuls of mixture onto prepared baking sheet; with back of spoon, spread thinly into 5-inch circles.

3. Bake 6 to 7 minutes. Immediately remove from cookie sheet; place, top side down, on inverted juice glasses. Mold to form wavy edges. (If chocolate cracks, gently press together with fingers.) Let stand about 30 minutes or until hard and completely cool.

4. Prepare CHOCOLATE COATING. With small brush, coat inside of cups with prepared coating. Refrigerate 20 minutes or until coating is set.

5. Meanwhile, prepare LEMON CREAM; spoon scant 1/2 cup LEMON CREAM into each cup. Garnish with shredded lemon peel, if desired. Cover; refrigerate leftover desserts.

Chocolate Coating

3/4 cup HERSHEY'S SPECIAL DARK Chocolate Chips or HERSHEY'S Semi-Sweet Chocolate Chips

1 teaspoon shortening (do not use butter, margarine, spread or oil)

Place chocolate chips and shortening in small microwave-safe bowl. Microwave at MEDIUM (50%) 45 seconds; stir. If necessary, microwave at MEDIUM an additional 15 seconds at a time, stirring after each heating, just until chips are melted when stirred.

Lemon Cream

1 package (4-serving size) instant lemon pudding
   and pie filling mix

1 cup milk

$1/8$ teaspoon lemon extract

$1^1/2$ cups frozen non-dairy whipped topping, thawed

Combine pudding mix, milk and lemon extract in small
bowl. Beat on low speed 2 minutes. Fold in whipped topping;
refrigerate 30 minutes or until set. Makes about $2^1/2$ cups
cream.

Viennese Chocolate Torte

Makes 10 servings

1/4 cup HERSHEY'S Cocoa

1/4 cup boiling water

1/3 cup shortening

3/4 cup sugar

1/2 teaspoon vanilla extract

1 egg

1 cup all-purpose flour

3/4 teaspoon baking soda

1/4 teaspoon salt

2/3 cup buttermilk or sour milk*

1/4 cup seedless black raspberry preserves

CREAM FILLING (recipe follows)

COCOA GLAZE (recipe follows)

MOUNDS Sweetened Coconut Flakes, toasted

*To sour milk: Use 2 teaspoons white vinegar plus milk to equal 2/3 cup.

1. Heat oven to 350°F. Lightly grease 15½×10½×1-inch jelly-roll pan; line pan with wax paper and lightly grease paper.

2. Stir together cocoa and boiling water in small bowl until smooth; set aside. Beat shortening, sugar and vanilla in medium bowl until creamy; beat in egg. Stir together flour, baking soda and salt; add alternately with buttermilk to shortening mixture. Add reserved cocoa mixture, beating just until blended. Spread batter in pan.

3. Bake 16 to 18 minutes or until wooden pick inserted in center comes out clean. Cool 10 minutes; remove from pan. Remove wax paper; cool completely. Cut cake crosswise into three equal pieces. Place one piece on serving plate; spread 2 tablespoons preserves evenly on top of cake. Spread half of CREAM FILLING over preserves. Repeat layering. Glaze top of torte with COCOA GLAZE, allowing some to drizzle down sides. Garnish with coconut. Refrigerate several hours. Cover; refrigerate leftover torte.

CREAM FILLING: Beat 1 cup whipping cream, 2 tablespoons powdered sugar and 1 teaspoon vanilla extract in small bowl until stiff. Makes about 2 cups filling.

Cocoa Glaze

2 tablespoons butter or margarine

2 tablespoons HERSHEY'S Cocoa

2 tablespoons water

1 cup powdered sugar

1/2 teaspoon vanilla extract

Melt butter in saucepan. Stir in cocoa and water. Cook, stirring constantly, until mixture thickens. Do not boil. Remove from heat. Whisk in powdered sugar gradually. Add vanilla and beat with whisk until smooth. Add additional water 1/2 teaspoon at a time until desired consistency.

Mocha Brownie Nut Torte

Makes 10 to 12 servings

1	cup (2 sticks) butter
1	package (4 ounces) HERSHEY'S Unsweetened Chocolate Premium Baking Bar, broken into pieces
4	eggs
1	teaspoon vanilla extract
2	cups granulated sugar
1	cup all-purpose flour
1	cup finely chopped pecans
1	package (8 ounces) cream cheese, softened
1	cup powdered sugar
1/2	cup chilled whipping cream
2	to 3 teaspoons powdered instant coffee
	CHOCOLATE GLAZE (recipe follows)

1. Heat oven to 350°F. Line bottom and sides of 9-inch round cake pan with foil, extending foil beyond sides. Grease foil.

2. Place butter and chocolate in medium microwave-safe bowl. Microwave at MEDIUM (50%) 1 minute; stir. If necessary, microwave an additional 15 seconds at a time, stirring after each heating, until chocolate is melted when stirred. Cool 5 minutes.

3. Beat eggs and vanilla in large bowl until foamy. Gradually beat in granulated sugar. Blend in chocolate mixture; fold in flour and pecans. Spread mixture in prepared pan. Bake 40 to 45 minutes or until wooden pick inserted in center comes out clean. Cool completely in pan on wire rack.

4. Use foil to lift brownie from pan; remove foil. Place brownie layer on serving plate. Beat cream cheese and powdered sugar in medium bowl until well blended. Beat whipping cream and instant coffee until stiff; gradually fold into cream cheese mixture, blending well. Spread over brownie layer. Cover; refrigerate until serving time.

5. Just before serving, prepare CHOCOLATE GLAZE. Drizzle generous tablespoon glaze over top and down sides of each serving.

CHOCOLATE GLAZE: Place 6 ounces (1 1/2 4-ounce bars) HERSHEY'S SPECIAL DARK Chocolate Premium Baking Bar and 1/2 cup whipping cream in small microwave-safe bowl. Microwave at MEDIUM (50%) 30 to 45 seconds or until chocolate is melted and mixture is smooth when stirred. Cool slightly. Makes 1 cup.

Holiday Treasure Cookies

Makes about 3 dozen cookies

1 1/2 cups graham cracker crumbs

1/2 cup all-purpose flour

2 teaspoons baking powder

1 can (14 ounces) sweetened condensed milk (not evaporated milk)

1/2 cup (1 stick) butter or margarine, softened

1 3/4 cups (10-ounce package) HERSHEY'S MINI KISSES BRAND Milk Chocolates

1 1/3 cups candy coated chocolate pieces

1 1/3 cups MOUNDS Sweetened Coconut Flakes

1 cup coarsely chopped walnuts

1. Heat oven to 375°F. Stir together graham cracker crumbs, flour and baking powder in small bowl; set aside.

2. Beat sweetened condensed milk and butter until smooth; add reserved crumb mixture, mixing well. Stir in chocolate pieces, candy coated chocolate pieces, coconut and walnuts. Drop by rounded tablespoons onto ungreased cookie sheet.

3. Bake 8 to 10 minutes or until lightly browned. Cool 1 minute; remove from cookie sheet to wire rack. Cool completely.

Creamy Cinnamon Chips Cheesecake

Makes 12 to 14 servings

1 1/2 cups graham cracker crumbs

1 cup plus 2 tablespoons sugar, divided

5 tablespoons butter, melted

2 packages (8 ounces each) cream cheese softened

1 teaspoon vanilla extract

3 cartons (8 ounces each) dairy sour cream

3 eggs, slightly beaten

1 2/3 cups (10-ounce package) HERSHEY'S Cinnamon Chips, divided

1 teaspoon shortening (do not use butter, margarine, spread or oil)

1. Heat oven to 325°F. Combine graham cracker crumbs, 2 tablespoons sugar and melted butter in medium bowl. Press crumb mixture evenly onto bottom and about 1 1/2 inches up side of 9-inch springform pan. Bake 8 minutes. Remove from oven.

2. Increase oven temperature to 350°F. Beat cream cheese, remaining 1 cup sugar and vanilla on medium speed of mixer until well blended. Add sour cream; beat on low speed until blended. Add eggs; beat on low speed just until blended. Do not overbeat.

3. Pour half of filling into prepared crust. Sprinkle 1 1/3 cups chips evenly over filling in pan. Carefully spoon remaining filling over chips. Place on shallow baking pan.

4. Bake about 1 hour or until center is almost set. Remove from oven; cool 10 minutes on wire rack. Using knife or narrow metal spatula, loosen cheesecake from side of pan. Cool on wire rack 30 minutes more. Remove side of pan; cool 1 hour.

5. Combine shortening and remaining 1/3 cup chips in small microwave-safe bowl. Microwave at MEDIUM (50%) 30 seconds; stir until chips are melted. Drizzle over cheesecake; cover and refrigerate at least 4 hours. Cover and refrigerate leftover cheesecake.

Easy Chip and Nut Gift Bread

Makes 3 small loaves

2 cups all-purpose flour

1 cup sugar

1 teaspoon baking powder

1 teaspoon salt

1/2 teaspoon baking soda

1 cup applesauce

1/2 cup shortening

2 eggs

1 cup HERSHEY'S Cinnamon Chips, HERSHEY'S SPECIAL DARK Chocolate Chips or HERSHEY'S Semi-Sweet Chocolate Chips

1/2 cup chopped walnuts

Powdered sugar (optional)

1. Heat oven to 350°F. Grease three 5¾×3¼×2-inch mini loaf pans.

2. Combine flour, sugar, baking powder, salt, baking soda, applesauce, shortening and eggs in large bowl. Beat on medium speed of mixer until well blended. Stir in cinnamon chips and walnuts. Divide batter evenly into prepared pans.

3. Bake 45 minutes or until wooden pick inserted in center comes out clean. Cool 10 minutes; remove from pans to wire rack. Cool completely. Sprinkle with powdered sugar, if desired.

Holiday Fudge Torte

Makes 8 to 10 servings

1 cup all-purpose flour

3/4 cup sugar

1/4 cup HERSHEY'S Cocoa

1 1/2 teaspoons powdered instant coffee

3/4 teaspoon baking soda

1/4 teaspoon salt

1/2 cup (1 stick) butter or margarine, softened

3/4 cup dairy sour cream

1 egg

1/2 teaspoon vanilla extract

FUDGE NUT GLAZE (recipe follows)

1. Heat oven to 350°F. Grease 9-inch round baking pan; line bottom with wax paper. Grease paper; flour paper and pan.

2. Stir together flour, sugar, cocoa, instant coffee, baking soda and salt in large bowl. Add butter, sour cream, egg and vanilla; beat on low speed of mixer until blended. Increase speed to medium; beat 3 minutes. Pour batter into prepared pan.

3. Bake 30 to 35 minutes or until wooden pick inserted in center comes out clean. Cool 10 minutes. Remove from pan to wire rack; gently peel off wax paper. Cool completely.

4. Prepare FUDGE NUT GLAZE.

5. Place cake on serving plate; pour glaze evenly over cake, allowing some to run down sides. Refrigerate until glaze is firm, about 1 hour. Cover; refrigerate leftover torte.

Fudge Nut Glaze

1/2 cup whipping cream

1/4 cup sugar

1 tablespoon butter

1 1/2 teaspoons light corn syrup

1/3 cup HERSHEY'S SPECIAL DARK Chocolate Chips or HERSHEY'S Semi-Sweet Chocolate Chips

3/4 cup chopped MAUNA LOA Macadamia Nuts, hazelnuts or pecans

1/2 teaspoon vanilla extract

1. Combine all ingredients except nuts and vanilla in small saucepan. Cook over medium heat, stirring constantly, until mixture boils. Cook, stirring constantly, 5 minutes. Remove from heat.

2. Cool 10 minutes; stir in nuts and vanilla.

Chocolate Peanut Clusters

Makes about 2 dozen candies

¹/₂ cup HERSHEY'S Milk Chocolate Chips

¹/₂ cup HERSHEY'S SPECIAL DARK Chocolate Chips or HERSHEY'S Semi-Sweet Chocolate Chips

1 teaspoon shortening (do not use butter, margarine, spread or oil)

1 cup unsalted, roasted peanuts or raisins

1. Place chocolate chips and shortening in medium microwave-safe bowl. Microwave at MEDIUM (50%) 1 minute; stir. If necessary, microwave at MEDIUM an additional 15 seconds at a time, stirring after each heating, just until chips are melted and mixture is smooth when stirred. Stir in peanuts.

2. Drop by teaspoons into a 1-inch diameter candy or petit four papers. Allow to set until firm, about 1 hour. Store in airtight container in cool, dry place.

Index

VOLUME MEASUREMENTS (dry)

1/8 teaspoon = 0.5 mL
1/4 teaspoon = 1 mL
1/2 teaspoon = 2 mL
3/4 teaspoon = 4 mL
1 teaspoon = 5 mL
1 tablespoon = 15 mL
2 tablespoons = 30 mL
1/4 cup = 60 mL
1/3 cup = 75 mL
1/2 cup = 125 mL
2/3 cup = 150 mL
3/4 cup = 175 mL
1 cup = 250 mL
2 cups = 1 pint = 500 mL
3 cups = 750 mL
4 cups = 1 quart = 1 L

VOLUME MEASUREMENTS (fluid)

1 fluid ounce (2 tablespoons) = 30 mL
4 fluid ounces (1/2 cup) = 125 mL
8 fluid ounces (1 cup) = 250 mL
12 fluid ounces (1 1/2 cups) = 375 mL
16 fluid ounces (2 cups) = 500 mL

WEIGHTS (mass)

1/2 ounce = 15 g
1 ounce = 30 g
3 ounces = 90 g
4 ounces = 120 g
8 ounces = 225 g
10 ounces = 285 g
12 ounces = 360 g
16 ounces = 1 pound = 450 g

DIMENSIONS

1/16 inch = 2 mm
1/8 inch = 3 mm
1/4 inch = 6 mm
1/2 inch = 1.5 cm
3/4 inch = 2 cm
1 inch = 2.5 cm

OVEN TEMPERATURES

250°F = 120°C
275°F = 140°C
300°F = 150°C
325°F = 160°C
350°F = 180°C
375°F = 190°C
400°F = 200°C
425°F = 220°C
450°F = 230°C

BAKING PAN SIZES

Utensil	Size in Inches/Quarts	Metric Volume	Size in Centimeters
Baking or Cake Pan (square or rectangular)	8×8×2	2 L	20×20×5
	9×9×2	2.5 L	23×23×5
	12×8×2	3 L	30×20×5
	13×9×2	3.5 L	33×23×5
Loaf Pan	8×4×3	1.5 L	20×10×7
	9×5×3	2 L	23×13×7
Round Layer Cake Pan	8×1½	1.2 L	20×4
	9×1½	1.5 L	23×4
Pie Plate	8×1¼	750 mL	20×3
	9×1¼	1 L	23×3
Baking Dish or Casserole	1 quart	1 L	—
	1½ quarts	1.5 L	—
	2 quarts	2 L	—